Lord Acton for Our Time

People for Our Time
A collection of books from Northern Illinois University Press

A list of titles in this collection is available at cornellpress.cornell.edu.

Lord Acton for Our Time

Christopher Lazarski

Northern Illinois University Press
An imprint of Cornell University Press
Ithaca and London

First published 2023 by Cornell University Press

Library of Congress Cataloging-in-Publication Data

Names: Lazarski, Christopher, author.
Title: Lord Acton for our time / Christopher Lazarski.
Description: Ithaca : Northern Illinois University Press, an imprint of Cornell University Press, 2023. | Series: People for our time | Includes bibliographical references and index.
Identifiers: LCCN 2022059469 | ISBN 9781501771712 (paperback) | ISBN 9781501771729 (epub) | ISBN 9781501771736 (pdf)
Subjects: LCSH: Acton, John Emerich Edward Dalberg Acton, Baron, 1834–1902—Political and social views. | Liberty—History. | Liberty—Philosophy.
Classification: LCC JC223.A35 L386 2023 | DDC 323.4401—dc23 /eng/20230111
LC record available at https://lccn.loc.gov/2022059469

To my sons Phil and Max

Contents

Introduction *1*

1 A Brief Biography *12*

2 The Theory of Liberty and Organic Liberalism *37*

3 Acton's History of Liberty *70*

4 Reception and Legacy *115*

Conclusion: Acton's Lessons for Today *135*

Notes *143*

Bibliography *159*

Index *167*

Introduction

"Power tends to corrupt and absolute power corrupts absolutely." Who does not know this maxim by Lord Acton (1834–1902), even if some of us are not aware who said it? It has become an element of common wisdom, both within and outside the English-speaking world, uttered frequently in the face of abuses of power and threats to freedom. If this were the only thought by which he would be remembered, he should be still considered as one of the most eminent political thinkers.

Lord Acton is not, however, a man of a single dictum. He wrote hundreds of essays and extensive book reviews and left rich correspondence, all of which include plenty of aphorisms as well as startling—often timeless—general views and observations relating to liberty, power, the state, democracy, liberalism, citizenship, religion, and so on. They allow us to better understand what makes the individual and society free or unfree, what makes the state and its regime friendly or unfriendly to civil society, and what makes us either citizens or subjects.

In the past he was often named a quintessential liberal, a historian (or even *the* historian) of liberty, and treated as the outmost authority on political freedom, even if his thought was only partly understood (see chapter 4). Today, he is no longer viewed as a "prophet" and "our contemporary," as the generation of World War II called him. Rather, he is seen as one of the classical liberals of the Victorian era, whose claim to distinction was his extraordinary, encyclopedic knowledge of modern history, his broad familiarity with political thought and theology, and his Catholicism (a thing unheard of among the nineteenth-century English liberals). As such, he has largely fallen into oblivion.

But is he really a figure of the past, respectable but outdated, a typical old-fashioned liberal, even if exceptionally well-read? Does he have no message for us who live in the twenty-first century?

The answer to these and similar questions is unequivocally no. Lord Acton is not passé: he can be a great teacher for current and future generations if they take the trouble to study him and uncover his wisdom. He belongs to a rare species of thinkers who have a capacity to penetrate into the nature of things—in his case this is particularly evident in matters of politics and social life. Where others only touched the surface, he reached beneath it and saw the hidden springs and wheels that move political and social reality. The power of his mind might be compared with that of Alexis de Tocqueville (1805–1859), a French thinker of the previous generation, one of his intellectual mentors, and a liberal of the same stripe. His capacity to go beneath the surface allowed him to make many observations that are striking in their originality and that are challenging to our well-established views and clichés.

Acton is also not an ordinary liberal—whether classical or otherwise—but that rare liberal of his kind whose concept of liberalism substantially differs from the meaning of the term in our time. He abhorred appeals to abstract principles (however lofty) and attempts to rearrange the existing order according to speculative theorems. Such an attitude usually sacrifices liberty for the sake of other values (typically equality) and leads to social engineering, if not outright coercion. Genuine liberalism must serve ordered liberty as its supreme goal. In practical terms this means respect for national tradition, not its rejection, and slow organic evolution, not a revolution. It also requires active citizens solving their own problems on a local level, not subjects dependent on the distant central government, however benevolent. Furthermore, Acton does not fetishize individual rights. The rights of individuals are counterbalanced by the "rights" of the community of which they are part. In other words, the community has the right to preserve itself and its way of life and ought not to be defenseless vis-à-vis the claims of the individual that violate its values and traditions (see chapters 2 and 3).

Finally, if Acton's writing on the history of liberty could be merely treated as good reading, interesting for lovers of history, his thought on liberty itself ought not to be underestimated. And certainly we must not ignore his warnings on the capacity of liberalism, democracy, and the modern state to degenerate into tyranny. On the contrary, we ought to listen carefully to his arguments that doctrinaire liberalism is in fact illiberal; that democracy naturally drifts into uniformity, intolerant of any distinction; that the modern state tends to become omnipotent; and that the combination of these three—constructivist liberalism, insufficiently balanced democracy, and an all-powerful state—constitute a deadly mix that could bring dire consequences for humanity: new forms of enslavement, more sinister than anything known in the past.

Shall we not listen to Acton's arguments rather than ignore them? This is not an abstract dilemma but a question that directly touches our everyday life. To illustrate this point, let us only consider such phenomena as the growing power of the state and its ever-ascending intrusiveness into our life, or think about the side effects of ubiquitous political correctness and the official and unofficial pressure that accompanies it. Are we really free if we are afraid of expressing our views in public, or if we may not control our children's upbringing and education? What is civil liberty worth, if it does not ensure freedom of worship but protects obscene behavior in public places? Can democracy be healthy if skills in deception and manipulation of the electorate are elevated to the dignity of science? (How else could we term political marketing and PR?) What can we say about a country that undermines the right to freedom of movement? Is it still liberal? In this context Acton's forewarnings acquire new urgency. Can we avoid the mistakes of the prewar generation and see Acton as a prophet for our generation before his predictions turn into reality?

As stated before, Acton is not a man of one maxim, so let us now glance at some of Acton's other dicta, beginning with the one that immediately follows his most famous quote, and then look at some of his ideas related to liberty and its history. This will give us the opportunity to judge for ourselves whether they accord with or challenge our convictions and opinions (quotations are from *Selected Writings of Lord Acton* [SWLA], *The Correspondence of Lord Acton and Richard Simpson*, and *Letters of Lord Acton to Mary, Daughter of the Right Hon. W. E. Gladstone*):

- "Great men are almost always bad men, even when they exercise influence and not authority." (*SWLA*, 2:383)
- "If happiness is the end of society, then liberty is superfluous. It does not make men happy." (*SWLA*, 3:490–91)
- "When a rich man becomes poor it is a misfortune, it is not a moral evil. When a poor man becomes destitute, it is a moral evil." (*SWLA*, 3:572)

- "Men cannot be made good by the state, but they can easily be made bad." (*SWLA*, 3:512)
- "Exile is the nursery of nationality, as oppression is the school of liberalism." (*SWLA*, 1:422)
- "Liberty has grown out of the distinction (separation is a bad word) of Church and State." (*Acton-Simpson Correspondence*, 2:251)
- "Liberty depends on the division of power. Democracy tends to unity of power." (*Letters of Lord Acton to Mary*, 98)
- "A common vice of democracy is disregard for morality." (*SWLA*, 3:557)
- "America has not solved the problem of reconciling democracy with freedom." (*SWLA*, 3:596)
- "A degenerate republicanism terminates in the total loss of freedom." (*SWLA*, 1:272)

Even this brief sample reveals to us the characteristic features of Acton's thought: originality often coupled with equivocal content. This impression is strengthened when we move to his more general thoughts:

- The belief that legitimate political power originates in the people did not emerge with liberalism but has held sway throughout the history of Western civilization, beginning at least with ancient Greece, and, except for a brief period of absolutism, has not been seriously challenged.
- The medieval church and great feudal lords constituted a counterbalance to royal authority; as long as they preserved their power, they prevented the rise of strong royal government and absolutism.

- The early modern period marked a significant regression in terms of civic liberty in comparison to the Middle Ages.
- English and American liberalism differed from continental liberalism in their origins, spirit, and policies.
- The liberal mainstream of continental Europe rests on a doctrinaire ideology, pursues abstract principles, and disregards the will and tradition as well as the rights of the people.
- The universal right to vote and other civil rights do not necessarily imply civic liberty, for they could mean omnipotent government, on the one hand, and subjects who exercise their citizenship only once every few years at the ballot box, on the other.
- Democracy has a capacity to be the best as well as the worst of regimes.
- Liberty ought to be the highest political end for governments and for true liberalism; all other principles, aims, and considerations (especially equality) are secondary in value.
- True liberalism and civic liberty are grounded in a people's sovereignty and developing political tradition; there must be no appeal to higher principles except for natural law. (Modern constitutions can play that role if they acknowledge human liberty and dignity and if they are well-balanced.)
- The US Constitution is a fraud, yet it is still best among existing constitutions as far as political liberty is concerned.

There is no doubt that some of these claims sound mysterious or controversial. They provoke many further questions rather than provide answers and require explanations, without which they lead to misapprehensions. Let us therefore ask, why is Acton's writing often confusing and full of riddles?

WHAT IS PRECIOUS is neither common nor easy to obtain. It requires effort on our part, usually great effort. Similarly, the treasures of Acton's wisdom, scattered throughout his writings, can be difficult to find and grasp. His writing does not make for easy reading. To understand the reason for it, consider the following four factors: First, Acton's erudition was legendary. Late in his life, his friends used him as a "walking encyclopedia," something like our search engines today. However, a side effect of his learning was his habit of making esoteric and equivocal references, assuming similar knowledge and understanding on the part of ordinary readers. In this he was mistaken, for how does one come to know who was "the most famous authoress of the Continent" to whom he attributed the maxim that "it is liberty which is ancient, and despotism which is modern"? And this reference can be considered an easy riddle. Much more difficult is, for example, his inaugural speech at Cambridge University, delivered in 1895, in which his erudition, abstruse hints, and hyperbole can intimidate and bewilder even an exceptionally well-educated person.

Second, Acton wrote over a span of about forty years, and it is therefore natural that his writing contains inconsistencies. He never published a book—including one on his greatest project, the history of liberty—in which he could present his views in a comprehensive manner. A casual reader can thus easily be confused by his seemingly contradictory remarks.

Third, Acton is often laconic in expressing his thoughts and ideas, as if he did not care about, or give much thought to, how they could be interpreted. This applies equally to an evaluation of relatively simple events as well as complex, long-term processes. For example, is he approving or disapproving of Plato and Aristotle when he says they aimed at "intelligent government"? Can we follow his train of thoughts on liberty in the West—from antiquity until the nineteenth century—when it is squeezed into two essays and one review? By comparison, Tocqueville wrote two thick volumes on democracy and liberty in America, that is, on one country over a span of roughly three hundred years.

Fourth, he frequently resorts to coded language, particularly when he assumes that the meaning of what he writes is apparent. He also knows how to be enigmatic when he prefers not to divulge his own attitude. The phrase "intelligent government" is a good example of the former, while his "minimalism" in evaluating the crimes of the French Revolution is a striking example of the latter.

Given these problems, can we expect to understand Acton's writings? How can we be sure we are not misinterpreting them? Are there methods that would allow us to decipher his messages as well as escape errors?

There is, naturally, no method that allows us to read Acton's mind (or anyone else's, for that matter). There are, however, simple ways to avoid mistakes in interpreting his thoughts that are available to thoughtful readers as well as to scholars who research him.

First, one should not begin one's acquaintance with Acton by reading essays in which he synthesizes broad topics. His inaugural speech at Cambridge and two lectures on the history of liberty illustrate this point well. All three suffer from the problems just listed and, additionally, make so many allusions assuming background knowledge and familiarity with the way Acton interprets the past that no "beginner," even if well-educated, can comprehend.

Second, a good introduction to Acton can be found in his early articles and reviews from the late 1850s and early 1860s when he began his writing career in the Catholic bimonthly *Rambler*, as well as in his most mature works, the *Lectures on Modern History*—

from chapter 3 onward—and *Lectures on the French Revolution*. They let the reader become familiar with how his mind operates and with his peculiar language and, if one is attentive, untangle some of his references, such as "the most famous authoress" (Madame de Staël). Furthermore, those early writings are helpful for learning how he encodes his meaning. After reading his chapter on Machiavelli, one has no doubt that in referring to an intelligent (or efficient) government Acton is implying not approval but sarcastic disdain, reflecting his contempt for top-down governments run by specialists and "jurists" who think they know better how to make people happy than the people themselves. Similarly, one learns that "pure democracy," "unlimited government," "centralization of power," and "equality as superior to liberty" are always pejoratives for Acton, while "conscience," "self-government," "higher law," and "liberty as superior to equality" are invariably positive terms for him. This in turn lets the readers uncover his attitudes toward various events, toward which he preferred to hide his opinions.

From what has been written so far, it is obvious that one ought to immerse oneself in Acton's writings in order to comprehend and appreciate his message and avoid basic mistakes in understanding his thought. It is true that his opinions evolved—particularly his view of the Catholic Church, which changed from enthusiasm to a nearly obsessive focus on its evil deeds; yet they remained remarkably consistent as far as liberty, its history in the West, and liberalism are concerned. Even his attitude toward the church itself did not change as much as it seemed to. With respect to politics, he viewed the church as having the mission of securing individual autonomy in the religious sphere and opposing state despotism, and as long as the church remained true to that mission, its role was positive. The trouble in understanding this simple message and thereby discovering Acton's true attitude toward the Catholic Church is that a reader must get through both his eulogies and critiques (some of which bordered on slander). Consequently, one ought to examine his writings in their entirety, not in fragments.

In addition to alerting attentive readers to resources available to them, scholars must apply the methodology that is appropriate for their fields. Practicing two disciplines, history and political science, the author of this book finds the methods of the historian's craft superior to those of a political scientist. Looking at Acton's thought through the lenses of theory neither seems helpful nor facilitates an objective evaluation. It results in viewing Acton as either a Pelagian, or a confused liberal, or a socialist in disguise, or even as an empty figure who mindlessly intones the word "liberty." A historian's methods, beginning with the stress on primary sources, their critical analysis, and an unbiased attitude that aims at objectivity as much as possible, seem to work much better.

In recreating Acton's theory and history of liberty, the author has made a fundamental (but obvious) assumption that Acton was an honest thinker who did not deliberately mislead his readers. Consequently, the author did not dwell on Acton's abstruse language, inconsistences, paradoxes, and contradictions, but searched for their logical explanations, assuming that various ideas and thoughts scattered throughout his writing can be put together into a coherent whole. This approach makes Acton's message transparent and lets him speak to us again in full might. Furthermore, it turns this book into a guide introducing interested readers to his original writings.

ACTON, ESPECIALLY IN his youth, was attracted by a variety of interests and wrote on many unrelated topics. Liberty, however, always played an important role in his writings, even if originally as a point of reference rather than a topic. Gradually it emerged as his principal passion, greater than any other theme or interest. Thus, liberty—how he understood it, what he thought was its foundation and necessary ingredients, as well as the history of its development in Western civilization—is the focus of this book. Specifically, the following chapters will first familiarize readers with Acton's life and his various pursuits and interests and then take a close look at his theory and history of liberty. Before the book concludes, chapter 4 will deal with the reception of his thought, a fascinating story in itself.

Acton was an ardent liberal who virtually identified the cause of liberty with that of liberalism. This book therefore analyzes his type of liberalism and, as promised, probes whether it can offer a solution to the crisis of liberal democracy in our own time.

1

A Brief Biography

Lord Acton's full name was John Emerich Edward Dalberg Acton. He usually introduced himself as John Acton, sometimes as John Dalberg-Acton. Born in Naples in 1834, he became the 8th Baronet of Aldenham (his family seat from the fourteenth century, located in England's West Midlands) after his father, Sir Richard Ferdinand, died. When Acton was thirty-five years old, Queen Victoria elevated him to a hereditary peerage; henceforth, he bore the title of the 1st Baron Acton. On his mother's side, his ancestors belonged to old German nobility. In 1810, his maternal grandfather was granted the title of Duke de Dalberg by Napoleon I; the duke's schloss in Herrnsheim (around Worms) was inherited by his daughter Marie Louisa, Acton's mother, and later became the second home of his grandson.

Distinguished family and international connections did not make John Acton an English aristocrat. Like his father, he was born abroad and had to go through the process of naturalization in the United Kingdom. His family was Catholic and his early education took place in Catholic institutions. On account of his religion, he was not admitted to Cambridge or Oxford; therefore, he received the equivalent of higher education in Munich under the supervision of a Catholic priest. Throughout his life, he remained an outsider in background, education, and faith, with the manners and appearance of a "continental gentleman."

There was probably one more factor that made him rather outré even in his own milieu: his childhood. His father died when he was three; his mother remarried when he was six and left him in the care of her Italian mother-in-law. Two years later, he was placed in a boarding school, moving from one place to another and hardly ever seeing his mother and grandmother. Letters from this time reveal a lonely boy who yearned to be with his mum. Although he "was putting on the brave face expected of young Englishmen," he occasionally revealed his true feelings, as evidenced by a letter to his mother sent from St. Mary's College in Oscott (1842): "I am very, very, very unhappy here and I beg you to come and fetch me as soon as possible." It was in this context that his most thorough biographer Roland Hill noted that "the English boarding school system was probably the worst form of education."

Acton only experienced family life at sixteen when his Bavarian tutor, Father Ignaz von Döllinger, substituted for his father and when he developed a warm relationship with his aristocratic Bavarian relatives. The Count and Countess von Arco-Valley (her mother was sister to Acton's maternal grandmother) had many children and accepted John as one of their own. Years later, in 1865, he married one of their daughters, Marie, and their villa in Tegernsee (located about thirty miles from Munich) was like his third home. His upbringing probably contributed to his future table manners: he could be either the most interesting and charming conversationalist or sit for hours with a stony face, keeping silent throughout, particularly if he was in a large company.

If Acton's childhood formed his personality, his stay in Munich (June 1850–December 1854) shaped his scholarly interests and lifelong passions. Acton rented room and board in the house of

Father Döllinger, the theologian and church historian. Döllinger imposed a rigorous schedule on the young man's training from early morning until night, inciting in him an interest in history and, through history, in theology and politics. It was then that he acquired his lifelong habit of reading one book per day and making notes, or at least leaving slips of paper in between pages he considered important. It is an open question whether Döllinger was responsible for not only Acton's insatiable thirst for books but also his inability to stop researching and begin writing. He always thought he needed additional reading and research. As for buying books, usually in cheap editions, he collected about seventy thousand volumes in Aldenham and the smaller libraries in his other residences.

Acton's higher education in history, his chosen field, as well as remedial study of Latin, Greek, and German, were supervised by Döllinger. At Munich University, where he had planned to study, he took only a few courses and never graduated. Döllinger also took care of Acton's intellectual development, recommending to him Alexis de Tocqueville (1805–1859) as a remedy for Thomas Babington Macaulay (1800–1859), the epitome of a Whig historian, and allowing him to continue his interest in Edmund Burke (1729–1797). These three—Döllinger, Tocqueville, and Burke—became Acton's intellectual staples in his youth and continued to exert influence on him thereafter, even when he quarreled with Döllinger and Burke or searched for points of difference with Tocqueville. Together they made him a thinker and a liberal of a unique kind, linking a belief in progress with respect for tradition; an appreciation for the role of the Catholic Church in history with an uncompromising censure of its faults; a love of liberty with an emphasis upon conscience, self-government, and citizenry; and the adornment of liberalism with contempt for and rejection of its doctrinaire currents.

DURING ACTON'S YEARS as a minor, the Aldenham estate was formally under the care of his mother but actually run by her husband, George Levenson-Gower, the 2nd Earl Granville, who was a distinguished Whig politician. Lord Granville treated the Aldenham manor as his second home and wanted to purchase it, thinking Acton would not live in the countryside. His stepson, however, politely rejected the offer but extended an invitation to Granville and his wife to stay in Aldenham for as long as they wished. It appears that he wanted to be the master of his estate and the manor.

Acton's estate covered more than six thousand acres but was heavily in debt. The new master was informed that he had to live on about one-tenth of his projected revenue, that is, about £1,000 a year. Despite the decreased land values, increased debt, bad stewardship, and generous grants Acton awarded causes he supported, the income from the estate allowed him to live comfortably for the next quarter-century, maintaining residences in Aldenham and Herrnsheim, as well as an apartment in London.

Foreign trips that Acton took in the 1850s began before he had settled down in Aldenham. He visited various cities in Europe, usually traveling with Döllinger during their summer vacations. Those trips with Döllinger occasionally continued even beyond Acton's study in Munich. In 1857, they both went to Rome, then still the capital of the Papal States. They were disappointed by the low level of scholarship among the Roman theologians and bad government in the Papal States. Although this did not immediately change Acton's view of the church, it probably had an impact on his future criticism of papacy and high hierarchy in general.

In 1853, still a student, Acton traveled to America as a member of the British delegation to the New York "Exhibition of the Industry of All Nations." His participation in the trip was arranged by his stepfather, who wanted to draw his stepson to politics.

America did not appeal to the tastes of nineteen-year-old Acton. He made some disparaging remarks about the country, its inhabitants, and its higher education. Commenting in his diary on Maine's law prohibiting liquor sales, he wrote, "Bureaucratic interference appears strange in such a free country." In New York City, he found that "there is little to be seen . . . ; it is not a fine city." As for table manners, he was "struck with the voraciousness with which they dispatched their dinner." On Harvard University, he noted that it was supported by private means. "The state, instead of contributing anything, claims a tax of 700 dollars a year. Its revenues . . . are comparatively great. Still, there is not enough to collect a fine library, nor to reward the professors well." As for the six hundred students who studied there, "they pay 80 dollars a year, and . . . pass for the most dissipated students in the Union."

On his way back to England, he—together with his mother and stepfather—dined with Queen Victoria and Prince Albert when their ships anchored in Holyhead, Wales. This gave him occasion to brag in a letter to Döllinger how much he had told the royal couple about America.

Acton's superficial view of America would change a few years later. As early as the mid-1860s, he realized that the United States was a prime example of civic liberty and the best practical application of his true, organic liberalism. He must have sensed it even during the visit, for he wrote to Döllinger, "There are much greater lessons to be learned here than I imagined and much more than I can as yet take advantage of. My ideas will be set in order by this journey, and I shall have gained a great interest in the country."

Three years later, in 1856, Acton took part in another trip at the instigation of his stepfather. Lord Granville headed the official British delegation to Russia that was to represent Queen Victoria at the coronation of Tsar Alexander II. Acton and his mother (Granville's wife) were among about twenty members of the delegation and their servants. As a young attaché, he took care of simple tasks and discussed the details of the coronation ceremony and its banquets and receptions. On his own, he engaged in some sightseeing in St. Petersburg, admiring Orthodox churches and noticing differences between Western and Russian cities. He left no Russian diary, but it is doubtful that his future negative view of Russia resulted from this trip.

Lord Granville tried to draw his stepson into politics not only by inviting him on state-sponsored foreign travels but also by encouraging him to run for public office. In 1859, he wanted Acton to run for a seat in the House of Commons. The Whigs had never had a good relationship with the Catholic Church and therefore with the Catholic electorate. Acton, coming from an old Catholic family, educated in Catholic institutions, and with good connections with church hierarchy (his quarrels with the church had not yet begun), presented to them an opportunity to win Catholic votes. Church leaders had similar feelings about Acton's candidacy, hoping he would act in the interest of the church and its faithful. Furthermore, he was wealthy enough to finance his campaign. Acton himself was not happy about getting involved in active politics (this coincided with the beginning of his work as a writer in and editor of Catholic journals), but he was unable to resist his stepfather's pressure.

The borough from which he was to run was located in Carlow, an overwhelmingly Catholic town in Ireland with about nine thousand inhabitants but only 236 electors. Granville believed that with about £700 for the campaign his stepson could win even without bribery. He had overestimated the cost: Acton won the election with a spend of only £500. Moreover, he did it without even appearing in Carlow. The crucial factors, however, were not his money or his personal campaign but the support of the local clergy and Cardinal Nicholas Wiseman, head of the Catholic Church in England. They had created an image of Acton among Carlow inhabitants as a defender of Catholicism and Irish causes. When he visited the town a month later, he was greeted enthusiastically by thousands of supporters, happy that he had defeated a Protestant (and Tory) rival.

The expectations of Carlow's Catholics and the church hierarchy for the new deputy were high, as was their subsequent disappointment with his work within and without the House of Commons. Acton was a passive MP, asking only three questions during his term. On Catholic issues, he voted together with three other Catholic MPs from Ireland, sometimes against a party line, but his inactivity was striking. Obviously Parliament procedure was not his cup of tea. Furthermore, the period between 1858 and 1865 was the time of his editorial work on the *Rambler* and *Home and Foreign Review*, during which he entered into an open conflict with the church hierarchy. Running in Carlow for a second term was thus out of the question, to his great relief. It seems the only positive outcome of his parliamentary experience was a long-lasting friendship with distinguished liberal politician and future four-time prime minister William E. Gladstone, with whom he shared an interest in theology, religion, morality, and politics. Gladstone's Anglicanism did not matter, while his anti-papal bias probably strengthened their bonds, even if Acton did not fully agree with him.

Acton's wish to be left alone and allowed "to settle down among [his] books" was not realized immediately after his term expired. Liberals from Bridgnorth, the borough of his residence (Aldenham), put forward his candidacy in the upcoming election (1856). But his electoral victory was illusory this time: he had won by just one vote, which ballot scrutiny turned into a defeat. This was not, however, the end of his parliamentary "career." On the recommendation of Prime Minister Gladstone, Queen Victoria gave him a peerage in 1869, and as Baron Acton, he gained a permanent seat in the House of Lords. His reluctance to participate in parliamentary politics did not change; his activity among the lords was just as "intensive" as it was among the MPs.

For Acton, the 1860s was filled with editorial work and Westminster experience, but it was personally important as well. In 1864, he was accepted by Marie Arco as her fiancé. Her decision was not obvious; she had hesitated for a few years. She was looking for affection, not talks about the strange ideas of which Acton was so fond. Further, Marie probably resisted him as a suitor because he was supported by her parents and seemed to take her for granted. What is more, she had reason to suspect that his feelings for her mother were greater than for her. (Hill implies that, back in the early 1850s, Acton's affection for Madame Arco was not entirely filial.) After her hesitation was finally overcome, they and her parents spent most of the time together, traveling throughout Italy. Their wedding took place in July 1865.

Acton was happy during his engagement to Marie, as his letters to Döllinger attest. Marie's portraits show her as a pretty woman with "bright blue eyes, a good complexion, and a lovely figure." Further, she was "sensible" and caring and later turned out to be a good mother. Acton, therefore, had every reason to be happy as a husband, and so he seemed to be. Hill speculates about a lack of passion in their marriage, calling it a marriage of convenience, but stresses that, in line with Victorian morality, they both did their best to be a good couple and good parents. Between 1866 and 1876 Marie gave birth to six children, four girls and two boys. Two of them died: a one-year-old boy in 1873 and a seven-year-old girl in 1881. (Acton's grief following the death of Lily was profound: he later requested to be buried next to her.) Their youngest, Jeanne, was "a backward child" who was given to fits of screaming and required her mother's constant care.

In later years, Acton's marriage suffered estrangement—they often lived in different residences. Hill suspects that Acton's pride was hurt by Marie's hesitation prior to their marriage, while she expected from him tenderness rather than intellectual intimidation, even if the latter was unintended. The estrangement turned into a crisis in the early 1890s, overcome only during the last years of Acton's life. We do not know the exact reasons for it, although Hill implies that it could have been due to infidelity on Marie's part.

Still, he was a good father and his children adored him. When he was at home (and he was often away for a long time), he took care of them no less than their mother did. "It was he who took them to the doctor or to the dentist . . . and who instilled the love of history in them by telling them stories." If they had trouble falling asleep, he would sing them lullabies. If they were naughty, however, he did not hesitate to chastise them with whips. Of his children, Marie, the oldest, was the closest emotionally to him and was apparently his favorite child; his second daughter, Anne Mary, shared his scholarly interest and was the closest intellectually. Richard Maximilian, the future 2nd Baron Acton, did not inherit his father's intellectual prowess and probably felt overwhelmed by it.

A Catholic Liberal

Upon his return from Munich to England, Acton was full of the ideas Döllinger had implanted in his mind relating to Christianity, the Catholic Church, modern science, liberalism, and liberty. From the beginning of 1858 to the end of 1870, a passion for reconciling Catholicism with the modern world, science, and liberalism dominated his work. At the same time, however, his passion for liberty itself grew systematically stronger until it gradually encompassed and eclipsed all other interests, ultimately becoming his life's passion.

When the young and enthusiastic Acton threw himself into the task of razing barriers between Catholicism and liberalism, he was not aware of the magnitude of his undertaking. At least since the Enlightenment, these two forces had been implacable enemies. For liberals, the church was the chief mainstay of the ancien régime, an epitome of tradition with its institutions, laws, privileges, and habits that for ages had sanctioned inequality and injustice in the society of estates. The church stood at the center of the world that had to be destroyed so that a new, better world could be built. The French *philosophes* maligned and ridiculed the church and faith with words, while their students attempted to annihilate it with force during the French Revolution. Liberal governments in Europe after the Congress of Vienna (1815) were far from sanctioning revolutionary violence, yet they had no intention of respecting the church's privileged position and autonomy. Thus, the conflict between them was natural.

Pius IX, history's longest reigning pope (1846–1878), had tried to change this situation at the beginning of his pontificate, attempting rapprochement with the modern world. After the painful experience of the revolutions of 1848, however, when he had to flee

Rome and spend two years in exile in the Kingdom of the Two Sicilies, he reverted to the old policy of confrontation rather than reconciliation with modernity. Furthermore, as a secular ruler in the Papal States, the pope was threatened by both liberalism and nationalism (then still hardly distinguishable) that aimed at abolishing old regimes and unifying Italy. The situation became acute in the early 1860s when French troops protected papal possessions, which were reduced to the region of Rome. It is therefore not surprising that the pope condemned "progress, liberalism and modern civilization" in his encyclical *Quanta Cura* and the *Syllabus Errorum* (1864).

Specific circumstances in England did not make Acton's task easier. The Catholic Church in the United Kingdom comprised either small circles of nobles who clung to pre-Reformation rituals and were fearful of any change or the poor and uneducated Irish suffering from centuries of discrimination and exploitation. Both groups were not ready to flirt with the emerging English liberalism, still under the strong influence of the Whiggish tradition (representing the landowning nobility and gentry and controlling Parliament, the Whigs were the chief force of English political tradition from the seventeenth century; see chapter 3). The Catholic hierarchy, then in the process of restoration after the blows of the sixteenth and seventeenth centuries, had to maneuver between those two groups and keep an eye on the so-called Oxford converts. They consisted of former Anglican priests and intellectuals who switched to Catholicism but preserved liberal sympathies. The symbolic head of this group was John Henry Newman (1801–1890), a future cardinal. The leaders of the Catholic Church in England, Cardinal Wiseman and his successor (from 1865), Archbishop Henry Manning, expected loyalty from the faithful both in defending the pope's temporal power and in serving English Catholicism.

Naturally, they also expected it from Acton, their well-born son whose Catholic credentials seemed impeccable.

Acton attempted his task as if he had not been aware of this deep-seated hostility and the conflicting interests at play. It is as though he believed (as he probably did) that this strife was based on misunderstanding and prejudice that investigation could clarify. Clarification could have dispelled enmity, allowing both sides to work together against conservative defenders of the old regime in the secular world and the old ways in the church. What were the grounds for Acton's great optimism?

First, he was convinced that the church had no reason to be afraid of modern science. Scientific truth about nature and the universe cannot contradict the fundaments of Christianity, a revealed religion: God, the author of creation, does not lie about it in His revelation. Truth about church history (Acton's domain), although at times unpleasant, does not weaken Christianity; on the contrary, truth can purify it of what is not essential to it. The last point was certainly the lesson Acton learned from Döllinger: his duty as a historian was to pursue truth and only truth, to the extent that it is knowable.

Second, Acton profoundly believed that Christianity and the church serve the cause of liberty (another lesson his professor taught him). The essence of Jesus's teaching is love, on the one hand, and, on the other, the liberty to accept or reject that love. The church ministered this teaching in antiquity by demanding autonomy for individuals in their relations to God, and then in the Middle Ages by constituting a counterbalance to state authority and by being an agent of civilization. Furthermore, the Catholic Church saved Christianity from splitting into national churches through which governments could control both spiritual and civil power. Although Acton admitted that the Renaissance papacy no longer played that role, his youthful zeal moved him to exempt the church from responsibility for the Reformation and even explained away Catholic persecution.

Consequently, Acton held that the church and liberalism, if purified from that which does not belong to their substance, have similar goals and therefore can work together. To that end, he exerted himself with a vengeance, devoting to this aim all his energy and talent, as well as substantial funds. The peak of this activity fell in the late 1850s and 1860s and ended soon after the First Vatican Council (1869–1870). During that time, he either cofinanced or substantially supported four journals while contributing to them as an author. These were the Catholic bimonthly *Rambler* (1858–1862) and the quarterly *Home and Foreign Review* (1862–1864) as well as two liberal journals aimed at a mainly Catholic audience: the weekly *Chronicle* (1867–1868) and the quarterly *North British Review* (1869–1871). Of the first two journals he was also a co-owner and served as coeditor.

Joining *Rambler* put Acton on a collision course with the church. The journal originally represented the views of the Oxford movement, but by increasingly discussing biblical scholarship and scientific challenges to creationism, as well as criticizing dogmatism in church teaching, it gradually evolved into a journal of liberal Catholic opinion. Thus, the conflict between the journal and Cardinal Wiseman had predated Acton's joining the *Rambler*. His contributions to aggravating that conflict were slight at first but grew year by year. He believed he had full freedom in matters that did not touch Catholic dogma and the pope's ex cathedra teaching. He particularly refused to compromise his integrity as a historian: whatever had been shameful in church history ought not be either hidden or sugarcoated but rather fully exposed. In his research, he increasingly began to notice immoral, even evil, deeds on the part of church hierarchy, especially the papacy. The full extent of his distrust and criticism would reveal itself in the late 1860s, but the first signs of disillusionment appeared earlier.

The leaders of the Catholic Church in England were shocked at the evolution of the *Rambler*'s editorial line. After informal warnings did not work, Cardinal Wiseman and other bishops condemned the journal in 1861. With de jure reverence, but in de facto defiance, the *Rambler* was closed down but carried on under the name *Home and Foreign Review*, with the same authors and policies. Wiseman consequently condemned it a year later. The quarterly continued on its way until a papal brief (March 1864) left no doubts that the church would not tolerate independence in scholarly work and publishing. The last issue of the *Review* in April 1864 contained Acton's article "Conflicts with Rome," in which he unrepentantly defended freedom of scholarly inquiry and rejected the thought of submitting truth to dogma. Closing the *Review* was thus the only solution that allowed him to "combine the obedience . . . to legitimate ecclesiastical authority, with an equally conscientious maintenance of the rightful and necessary liberty of thought."

Acton's next two attempts at high-quality journalism, the *Chronicle* and the *North British Review*, were equally short-lived. Although both, particularly the *North British Review*, represented quality "comparable to the best in Victorian periodical journalism," they needed wealthy sponsors to maintain them. Acton was not wealthy enough to do it alone; seeing the futility of his efforts, he was increasingly dejected and so let the *Review* fall.

The First Vatican Council was the last occasion for Acton to put all his passion into the service of liberal Catholicism. Pius IX had revealed his intention of calling a general council a few years earlier, and that initiative immediately roused protests in liberal Catholic circles in France and Germany. The council was to discuss many issues, but the proclamation of papal infallibility was to be one of its main aims. Acton could not disagree more with this idea.

By 1870, his view of church authority in the modern period was entirely negative. The church had betrayed its vocation, both in politics and in its spiritual mission. Instead of being an agent of freedom, it began to compete for worldly power. What is more, to fight its enemies, it resorted to persecution, torture, and executions, and it justified its evil deeds according to the good ends those deeds allegedly furthered. Papal infallibility seemed to Acton to be in line with this shameful tradition. It was indefensible in theology and sinister in politics because it raised the worst aspect of the life of the church—uncontrolled, arbitrary power in both spiritual and political domains—to the dignity of dogma.

During the council, Acton spent about half a year in Rome opposing the idea he abhorred. He used three tactics. He attempted, first, to organize an opposition among the council's participating bishops; second, to raise public opinion against defining papal infallibility as a dogma; and, third, to mount political pressure on the church. When it came to the first goal, the delegates who opposed papal infallibility, a minority, opposed it for a variety of reasons, some of them incompatible; they had no links among themselves; and they spoke different languages (though they all knew Latin). Acton networked them: his Roman rental apartment served as the headquarters of the anti-infallibilists. In church history, this was an extraordinary role for a layperson to play. Regarding the second aim, he took advantage of inside information provided by council delegates and forwarded it to anonymous authors, who then wrote letters signed by "Quirinus" and published them in the *Allgemeine Zeitung* newspaper in Augsburg. The letters—most of them authored by Döllinger—were sensational and as such were translated and published in many languages. Finally, because infallibility touched upon the question of the loyalty of Catholic subjects to their states, Acton hoped European governments, especially those of the United Kingdom, France, Austro-Hungary, and Prussia, would exert pressure on the pope to give up the idea. In this aim, Acton achieved no notable success.

Ultimately, the pope had his way, and the dogma of infallibility was overwhelmingly approved by the bishops: 535 votes for the new dogma, two against. However, the dogma as defined by the council was far from that which had aroused so much fear in liberal circles and Acton himself. The pope is infallible only when he speaks ex cathedra ("from the chair of Peter") in order to define church "doctrine regarding faith and morals." He is therefore not infallible in his political decisions or ordinary pronouncements. As for evaluation of Acton's work against papal infallibility, the British Minister of Foreign Affairs Lord Clarendon poignantly summarized it: the pope "stood alone against all the representation of the Catholic powers and all the opposition bishops plus Acton, who is worth them all put together."

Acton's activity in Rome during the church council and the closing of the *North British Review* ended his work in the field of liberal Catholicism. His past haunted him, however. In 1874, Britain's Prime Minister William E. Gladstone—also Acton's friend—published a pamphlet, *The Vatican Decrees in Their Bearing on Civil Allegiance*. During the council, Gladstone received many messages from his friend predicting the dire consequences of defining infallibility as a dogma and urging him to act against it. Gladstone preferred to ignore those warnings and followed the counsel of Britain's diplomatic representatives to be neutral; a few years later, he decided to use them as evidence that cast doubt on the civil loyalty of the Catholics. How could Catholic citizens be loyal to their states if the pope claims infallibility? The problem was serious in view of the recent removal of various disabilities that had been imposed on Catholics and their legal equality with other English subjects.

Acton felt obliged to counter his friend's thesis publicly. In an open letter to Gladstone published in *The Times*, he claimed that the new dogma did not change anything. Even before the council, the pope had had the authority to excommunicate and "depose Princes" and, although not a dogma, this papal prerogative had been treated in Rome as an article of faith. Instead of arguing against infallibility, Gladstone should have addressed the real problem of the church, namely, the perverted morality that absolves evil conduct for the sake of religion. Acton illustrated it by reminding readers of a medieval rule that killing an excommunicated person was not murder; that Pope Pius V had excommunicated Queen Elizabeth I and "commissioned an assassin to take her life"; and that his successor had approved the massacre of the Huguenots on the Night of St. Bartholomew. He also provided some examples of Catholic defiance against papal decisions to show once again that modern government had no reason to doubt the civil loyalty of their Catholic subjects.

What Acton probably planned as one letter ultimately turned into a series of four letters, published between November 8 and December 9, 1874. The first provoked the protests of Catholics and demands that he substantiate his accusations. In response, he restated his previous claims and added new examples of church misconduct and crimes, especially those that defended papal temporal power. Remaining unapologetic as far as his interpretation of facts was concerned, he still maintained that revealing the dark side of ecclesiastical history did not damage the church itself.

The letters to *The Times* got Acton into trouble with Archbishop Manning, who denounced him in Rome and demanded from him a formal statement of his adherence to the new dogma. In two letters to the archbishop, Acton used all his talents for abstruse writing to avoid directly addressing the issue, and finally, in a third, he denied the archbishop the right to ask a lay person such questions. Acton clarified the orthodoxy of his faith with the bishop of his own diocese, after which church authorities did not trouble him. On the contrary, with the passing of time, the church began to view him as a faithful son, particularly after Cardinal Manning's death in 1892. Döllinger, however, suffered more severe consequences as a priest. Because he refused to accept the new dogma, he was defrocked. Ultimately, he sympathized with and influenced (though did not join) the Old Catholic Church, a new denomination established in protest against the decrees of the First Vatican Council.

The Madonna of the Future

As mentioned in the introduction, liberty occupied a prominent place in everything Acton wrote. Topics varied, but liberty was always the key reference point, one that separated right from wrong, good from evil. His original enthusiasm about the Catholic Church resulted from his appreciation of its role in the growth of freedom, especially in antiquity and the Middle Ages. His increasing critique of the church and growing hostility to ecclesiastical hierarchy, in particular the papacy, had exactly the same roots: upon a closer look, the church he had admired so much turned out to be corrupt, in pursuit of worldly power, and therefore betraying its mission, of which liberty was an essential ingredient. For Acton, the time after the Vatican Council, without editorial and political burdens, was finally favorable for focusing on his passion. Yet the plan to focus on liberty and write its history did not occur to him suddenly but rather emerged gradually.

After the Vatican Council, Acton suffered a period of dejection. More than a decade of his work had been in vain. The Catholic Church and liberalism had not come closer to each other, and instead the gap between them had widened. It was obvious to him that this goal had to be abandoned. Furthermore, in the early 1870s, Acton had many projects: he still seemed to aim at exposing the church's fraud and misdeeds. Döllinger tried to dissuade his pupil from writing on so many topics and advised him to write a book instead, the sooner the better. By his prediction, if Acton did not write it by the age of forty—that is, by 1874—he never would.

Despite the variety of topics that interested him in the 1870s, Acton increasingly focused on the history of liberty. He began to collect and study primary sources and other evidence, as well as historical works relevant to his subject. Brief outlines of the future book were ready by 1877 when he offered two public lectures published as "The History of Freedom in Antiquity" and "The History of Freedom in Christianity." His review of Thomas Erskine May's *Democracy in Europe*, published in 1878, supplements the lectures and extends Acton's perspective to the nineteenth century. An oft-quoted conversation with his friend James Bryce (in fact a passionate outburst by Acton) showed that by 1882 he had the book ready in his mind, even if he had failed to put it down on paper:

> Twenty years ago, late at night, in his library at Cannes, he expounded to me his view of how such a history of Liberty might be written, and in what ways it might be made the central thread of all history. He spoke for six or seven minutes only; but he spoke like a man inspired, seeming as if, from some mountain summit high in the air, he saw beneath him the far-winding path of human

> progress from dim Cimmerian shores of prehistoric shadow into the fuller yet broken and fitful light of the modern time. The eloquence was splendid, but greater than the eloquence was the penetrating vision which discerned through all events and in all ages the play of those moral forces, now creating, now destroying, always transmuting, which had moulded and remoulded institutions, and had given to the human spirit its ceaselessly-changing forms of energy. It was as if the whole landscape of history had been suddenly lit up by a burst of sunlight. I have never heard from any other lips any discourse like this nor from his did I ever hear the like again.

If he had collected evidence and worked out the general vision of the project and if "he did have a masterpiece in him," as one of his reviewers had recently said, we then could ask: Why did he not write it? Why did he abandon the topic he loved so much? Why did his "History of Liberty" remain "the greatest book that never was written"?

There is no one answer to these questions. To understand the reasons for his failure—if we leave aside some radical explanations, ranging from a lack of intellectual courage to a lack of intention to write it—we have to consider three main factors: first, the high scholarly standards that the project was to meet; second, his belief in universal ethics and his stern morality, together with his idea of history as "a hanging judge"; and, third, his personal problems in the 1880s and early 1890s.

As regards high scholarly standards, Acton strongly believed that true history must be based, first of all, on primary sources that are hidden in various archives and awaiting discovery. Throughout his life, beginning with the years in Munich, he "hunted" for such sources in various places in Europe, especially in Rome. His history of liberty—essentially a history of Western civilization with freedom as its central theme—was designed to meet this fundamental requirement of a sound historical work. As if this criterion was not sufficiently prohibitive, he imposed another: it was to take advantage of the most recent scholarship on that topic. Although Acton continued his habit of reading one book a day, he was unable to keep up with historical scholarship, while, as we know, he had not been taught to stop research and begin writing: "The more he read . . . the more he wished to read."

With regard to ethics, in Acton's theory of liberty, conscience and morality played a central role (see chapter 2). Being God-given, ethical fundaments are the same for all people, regardless of time and circumstances: "Opinions alter, . . . creeds rise and fall, but the moral law is written on the tablets of eternity." If so, a historian's duty is not only to research the past but also to morally evaluate the conduct of historical figures, in particular great figures, especially when their crimes include assassination and murder. Moreover, he insisted that the "great men [who] are almost always bad men" be judged more severely than ordinary culprits. Historians, however, tend to do the opposite, explaining away their crimes by political ends, and, what is worse, they often resort to hero worship: "First, the criminal who slays; then the sophist who defends the slayer." Aware that intellectual trends were against him, Acton chose to be silent rather than to go against the tide. Only years later did he vent his view forcefully and successfully in his inaugural speech at the University of Cambridge (see chapter 4).

Finally, the serious personal problems Acton experienced in the 1880s certainly had an impact on his creativity. In addition to his marriage crisis, he faced increasing financial problems that bordered on bankruptcy. To reduce the cost of living, the Acton family moved to the French Riviera in 1878 and rented out Aldenham; he ceased renting his apartment in London in 1880 and later sold the schloss in Herrnsheim. He sold his library in 1890 and not much later the family jewelry.

Put together, all those problems proved to be overwhelming. Acton published less and less (he wrote little in the 1870s, still less in the 1880s) and kept postponing his greatest project, referring to it as early as 1879 as the "Madonna of the Future," that is, a work that is never attempted.

Regius Professor

The dire state of Acton's finances led him to think about a government position: perhaps a post in Gladstone's last cabinet, or at least a diplomatic post in a British embassy in Europe. Prussia or Bavaria were his preferred choices. The premier did not help his friend in this way but arranged a sinecure for him at the royal court. In 1892, Acton was appointed to the position of the lord-in-waiting. It did not require much effort on his part: he occasionally charmed Queen Victoria at meals and spent most of his time reading books in the court library. For a time, the position saved him from bankruptcy and later helped him to obtain another post that was much more suitable: the Regius Professor of Modern History at the University of Cambridge. The queen liked him and, in spite of his Catholicism and lack of formal academic qualifications, agreed to appoint him to one of the two most prestigious positions for modern historians in England (the second being at the University of Oxford) when Lord Rosebery, Gladstone's successor, submitted his candidacy in February 1895.

Acton's biographers agree that the six years of professorship at the University of Cambridge was one of the happiest periods in his life. He liked what he was doing—teaching students, in addition to reading books, turned out to be his favorite task—and gained financial stability that saved him from poverty. The inaugural lecture at Cambridge was a great success—in spite of its difficult content and it raising not necessarily popular themes on morality when evaluating the past—the audience instantly recognized that a great man had arrived at Cambridge.

Acton had a charismatic personality that shined fully at Cambridge and spellbound his audience, including other professors, who often attended his lectures. He had a "forbiddingly Victorian" appearance, as Hill expressed it, with "a full black beard that turned grey in his last years, brilliant blue eyes, a fine resonant voice, and the beautiful manners of a patrician." One of his students wrote about even more striking characteristics of Professor Acton and the impression he had made during his classes:

> There was a magnetic quality in the tones of his voice, and a light in his eye, that compelled obedience from the mind. Never before had a young man come into the presence of such intensity of conviction as was shown by every word Lord Acton spoke. It took possession of the whole being, and seemed to enfold it in its own burning flames. . . . It was perhaps this conviction that gave to Lord Acton's Lectures their amazing force and vivacity. He pronounced each sentence as if he were feeling it . . . and uttering it with measured deliberation. His feeling passed to the audience, which sat enthralled. It was in truth an emotional performance of the highest order, . . . a wonderful work of art, such as in all likelihood will never again be witnessed.

Acton was generous in sharing his time with students, giving them advice and providing them with not only a list of recommended reading but also the books on the list. One who consulted him on a matter "would probably find on his arrival home that Acton's servant had preceded him with a pile of books in half a dozen of languages, and a note stating that more would follow."

He taught two courses at Cambridge. The first was on the French Revolution, offered during the academic years of 1895 and 1897 and repeated from 1897 to 1899. The second was on modern history, about which he lectured from 1899 to 1901. Additionally, he initiated the foundation of the Trinity Historical Society, of which he became the president. The society attracted many students who at first were "a little awed by their President's weight of learning. But their shyness soon wore off." He certainly breathed new life into the study of history at the university.

The last years of Acton's life were devoted to yet another formidable task: editing a multivolume series on modern history, beginning with the Renaissance. Cambridge University Press proposed to him in 1896 that he become the editor of original works on history and, to lend more prestige to this enterprise, that he write a large part of them, at least in the first volume. The proposal was too tempting for Acton to refuse: it would give him a chance to finally implement many of his ideas on how "scientific" history should be written. Acton dismissed the treatment of history as a handmaid of politics and diplomacy (thus serving the transient national interest), an idea that still reigned at Cambridge. He aimed at universal history that shows long-term processes without regard for national borders or religious affinity and is written with objectivity. Whether by an English or a French person, a Catholic or a Protestant, history should be written in the same way, with no trace of the nationality or denomination of the authors.

Owen Chadwick, one of Acton's successors as Chair of the Regius Professor, wrote that the task Acton took upon himself "was not a sinecure." A vast correspondence with prospective authors, patient explanations of his ideas about the series, arguments that he had to employ in order to convince others to participate, and his effort to obtain outside funds (he found too meager the honorarium that the publisher offered to pay the authors) show how much work he had to perform. It was probably this work, not the teaching, that contributed to the deterioration of his health. Gouty arthritis that "had gone to the whole system" ended his work at Cambridge in the spring of 1901. He spent the last year of his life under the care of his daughters and wife in Tegernsee. He died on June 20, 1902, and was buried two days later in a local cemetery. His grave exists no longer: it was razed to the ground after World War II.

2

The Theory of Liberty and Organic Liberalism

Acton never wrote his own theory of liberty. What he left are scattered remarks on what he considered important for the foundation and growth of liberty in the past and what he deemed threatening to it. In their raw forms, these remarks are like pieces of a puzzle rather than a complete concept. He also left several definitions of liberty but did not take care to arrange them in some order. Acton's theory of liberty is therefore like his history of liberty: unwritten and known only in bits that at first glance do not always seem to be clear or to cohere.

Actonian scholars claim, however, that his history of liberty was fully thought-out—an unwritten masterpiece hidden in his mind—and sketched out in two essays on liberty as well as being hinted at in others, or revealed in outbursts, such as the one in Cannes that his friend James Bryce mentioned. We might presume that the same pattern applies to his theory of liberty, likewise worked out in his head but not poured out on paper. After all, his history of liberty could not be consistent without some theoretical grounding. Furthermore, although we do not have a complete theory, we do have many of its elements. Acton mentioned political ideals and virtues whenever he discussed aspects of freedom. Because such remarks and hints about liberty frequently occur in his writing, he did in fact provide enough of them to be compiled into a coherent whole. Directly or indirectly, he does say which political principles are the highest and which are not (or ought not to be); how they can be achieved; and how, in fact, they were accomplished in some places in the past.

Acton's theory of liberty is intimately linked to his notion of liberalism. On this topic he seems inconsistent as well. On the one hand, he worshipped liberalism and made it the most noble trend in Western history; on the other, he mercilessly attacked some of its principles, policies, and thinkers, especially those of continental liberalism. Yet, as with his theory of liberty, his seemingly erratic thoughts on liberalism can be put into a remarkably consistent whole if we recognize that he refers to two liberalisms, not one, differing from each other in their origins, priorities, and aims. Acton's fault seems to lie in his overestimation of his readers' knowledge and their capacity to comprehend his ideas. His views on liberty and liberalism, however, have remained valid up to our own times and can help us to sort out our own dilemmas.

The Core Elements of Political Liberty

Let us begin with Acton's statements on liberty that raise no doubt or leave little room for equivocal interpretations and then move on to more complex accounts. In his seminal essay on liberty in antiquity, he forcefully affirms that "liberty is not a means to a higher political end. It is itself the highest political end." As if he wished to dispel any misapprehension in this respect, in his lectures on the French Revolution written in the last years of his life he further elaborates that "the end of government is liberty, not happiness, or prosperity, or power, or the preservation of an historic inheritance, or the adaptation of national law to national character, or the progress of enlightenment and the promotion of virtue." All those aims are secondary, and the government that makes them superior to liberty must by necessity resort to social engineering and therefore becomes illiberal.

Liberty as the supreme aim of politics should be understood exactly as Acton expressed it: a goal to be pursued; an objective that evolves and matures together with a polity's natural development. In another essay, Acton describes this process this way: "Liberty is the term and aim of all government, not its principle and foundation. It should be present in germ at the foundation of the state, and should grow with its growth. The test of good government is the healthy development of liberty, not its present attainment. It must grow up harmoniously with the state of society, with the relations of classes to each other, and with the manners, customs, and legislation of the community." In yet another passage, he stresses the slowness of that process: "Liberty is a plant of slow growth and late maturity, and belongs only to nations that have reached their prime and have not approached decay."

This process of development is further illuminated in what is perhaps Acton's most important declaration on political liberty, made when he discussed liberty in ancient Israel: "The example of the Hebrew nation laid down the parallel lines on which all freedom had been won—the doctrine of national tradition and the doctrine of the higher law; the principle that a constitution grows from a root, by process of development, and not of essential change; and the principle that all political authorities must be tested and reformed according to a code which was not made by man." This passage is so essential that it requires some comments.

Acton stressed that ancient Israelites did not have a central government for a long time after their arrival in the Promised Land. They lived in a loose confederation of tribes and clans, their elders (judges) being the natural authority of each. This shaped their national tradition: self-reliance and power that were not imposed from the top but came from within, as their own. (Acton always insisted that the ultimate source of legitimate power lies with the people, provided they obey higher divine law.) This was clearly a liberty "present in germ at the foundation of the state," as he had postulated. Furthermore, when the Hebrew monarchy was finally established in 1047 BC, it was constrained by the tradition and legislative power that belonged only to God (later inscribed in the Torah). Acton appreciated this so much that he considered the Hebrew polity to be the beginning of political liberty in Western civilization.

For Acton this was a universal declaration, applicable not only to ancient Israel but to all polities, regardless of time and place ("the parallel lines on which all freedom had been won"). The Hebrew notion of liberty is important precisely because of the discovery of fundaments on which political liberty rests.

According to him, liberty requires a national tradition—with at least elemental freedoms at its foundation, naturally—and an organic evolution that excludes revolutionary changes. He reiterates this point and further argues for it in another place: "Polity grows like language, and is a part of a people's nature, not dependent on its will. [It] . . . can be . . . modified, . . . but . . . cannot be subverted . . . by the people itself without an act of suicide. . . . Revolution is a malady, a frenzy, . . . sometimes fatal to its existence, often to its independence. . . . It is not conceivable that a nation should arbitrarily and spontaneously cast off its history, reject its tradition, abrogate its law and government."

Acton also postulates a higher law, "not made by man." He abhorred speculative politics and its arbitrary principles—this was his main charge against continental liberalism—yet he insisted on the necessity of higher law that circumscribes the government and lets the people distinguish right from wrong and good from evil, even if the process of recognition takes centuries, as it did, for example, in the case of slavery. Of divine origins, natural law underwent a gradual secularization in modern times, turning into constitutional law, a process that Acton ultimately approved. This arbitrary element is indispensable in a regime that appreciates ordered freedom, but it is the only such element. National tradition and its organic growth cannot be challenged and changed by any other principle, if liberty is to be not crushed but preserved.

Acton places liberty at the center of his notion of politics. To make it more concrete, he stresses national tradition—and its organic growth—and higher law as its fundaments. Yet this concept of liberty still hangs in the air unless there is another ingredient—self-government. It is only with this element that his theory ceases to be abstract and acquires a practical dimension.

Self-government in Acton's thought is virtually synonymous with liberty. His claim that "the end of government is liberty" runs parallel to "self-government is the end of all government." Other words of his on this topic include the following: liberty's "characteristic sign and manifestation is self-government"; "self-government [is] the only secure basis of all freedom, whether political or religious"; "liberty equals self-government"; and "the point at which they [civil and religious liberties] unite, the common root from which they derive their sustenance, is the right of self-government."

According to Acton, self-rule and its essential role in the advancement of freedom are visible throughout Western history, but nowhere more than in America. In his view, American settlers came to a virgin land and built their polity on their own, with nearly no assistance from the distant metropolis. They did it in their daily struggle with nature—their survival depended on it—and in resolving countless mundane problems in their communities. Starting in a parish, continuing in the town and county, and ending with a colony, they gradually built their government. In this process, citizens were born, free, legally equal and in control of their own affairs. Their citizenhood was not a gift of a benevolent ruler but a treasure that they earned through their own efforts. The American Revolution completed this process by winning sovereignty for America and constructing a federal government for the former colonies, civic liberty for the citizens, and civil rights for the free inhabitants (the issue of slavery will be addressed separately).

Acton's view of self-government allows us to better grasp what he meant by liberty and what he cherished as its ideal. Liberty is not an incantation but a political reality arranged by citizens who take charge of their lives in both their private and public dimensions. It is the order in which the state belongs to its citizens, not the other way around. Acton always stressed that legitimate power (sovereignty) originates in the people, and that strong self-government is the best expression of this rule.

If the state controls the people, then we are dealing with subjects rather than citizens. It is so not only in arbitrary forms of government but also in liberal regimes when they have omnipotent governments, disrespect intermediary bodies—such as the church, provinces, towns, professional corporations, business organizations, educational institutions, and, ultimately, family—and reduce the exercise of citizenship to the act of voting every few years.

Acton's ideal of liberty is thus intimately linked to *civic* liberty. Its core elements are self-government and active citizens. This forms a communal dimension of his concept of liberty. That dimension is supplemented by an individual dimension, the freedom of the individual, or *civil* liberty.

Acton left several statements that let us better grasp his understanding of liberty. The first is an extension of the quotation already cited earlier: "The end of government is liberty, not happiness, or prosperity, . . . that the private individual should not feel the pressure of public authority, and should direct his life by the influences that are within him, not around him." In another remark Acton links freedom and individual rights even more strongly: "By liberty I mean the assurance that every man shall be protected in doing what he believes is his duty against the influence of authority and majorities, custom and opinion." On the surface, this notion appears similar to the standard liberal view on individual rights vis-à-vis government, majority, and tradition. Acton, however, is not like John Stuart Mill (1806–1873), who makes freedom of individuals nearly absolute (except when they pose a physical threat to others), or Immanuel Kant (1724–1804), who links it with the imperatives of practical reason. No, for Acton individual freedom is intimately bound with morality. Liberty is not "the power of doing what we like, but the right of being able to do what we ought." This clearly Catholic understanding of freedom brings us to the question of conscience.

Acton calls conscience "the audible voice of God, that never misleads or fails, and that ought to be obeyed always." Since conscience is "something divine in human nature," each of us has the right to follow its dictates and be unhindered by others in fulfillment of our duties. Furthermore, freedom of conscience is a superior right that may not be challenged by any power, while "all other liberty" serves to protect it. Acton treats it as "the birthright of man" and "the secret essence of the Rights of Man." Ultimately, he correlates liberty and conscience: "The proper name for the rights of conscience is liberty." Consequently, he places conscience and its corollary, morality and the right to follow it—in other words, individual rights—at the core of his notion of liberty.

If we now survey all the core principles and ingredients of liberty discussed so far, we can arrange them in the following three groups, all complementary and equal in value: liberty, national tradition (and its organic growth), and higher law; liberty, self-government, and citizens; and liberty, conscience-morality, and individual rights. All three have liberty as their aim, while all other elements in them are necessary conditions for liberty to develop and flourish and become ordered liberty. Figure 1 graphically presents the essence of Acton's theory of liberty.

Looking at it, we can better understand why Acton was intransigent in his emphasis on the moral evaluation of the past, that is, on treating history as the "hanging judge" (see chapter 4). This was not a side issue, irrelevant to the historian's craft, but a fundamental note in his notion of liberty. First, conscience and morality play a crucial role in it; and second, higher law and conscience are either transmitted to us by the "infallible voice of God in man" or are discovered by reason. "The moral law is written on the tablets of eternity"; it is therefore known to all, and villains cannot claim ignorance. Unlike other historians, Acton could not give up the moral evaluation of great figures of the past and practice "hero worship" without betraying the basic elements of his notion of liberty (see chapter 4).

To complete the key part of Acton's theory of liberty, we must add one more element that lies at its heart: Providence and its upholding of liberty. Acton claims that liberty is "the central thread of all history" and its unifying principle exactly because of divine will. "The world exhibits the hand of Providence . . . not by being

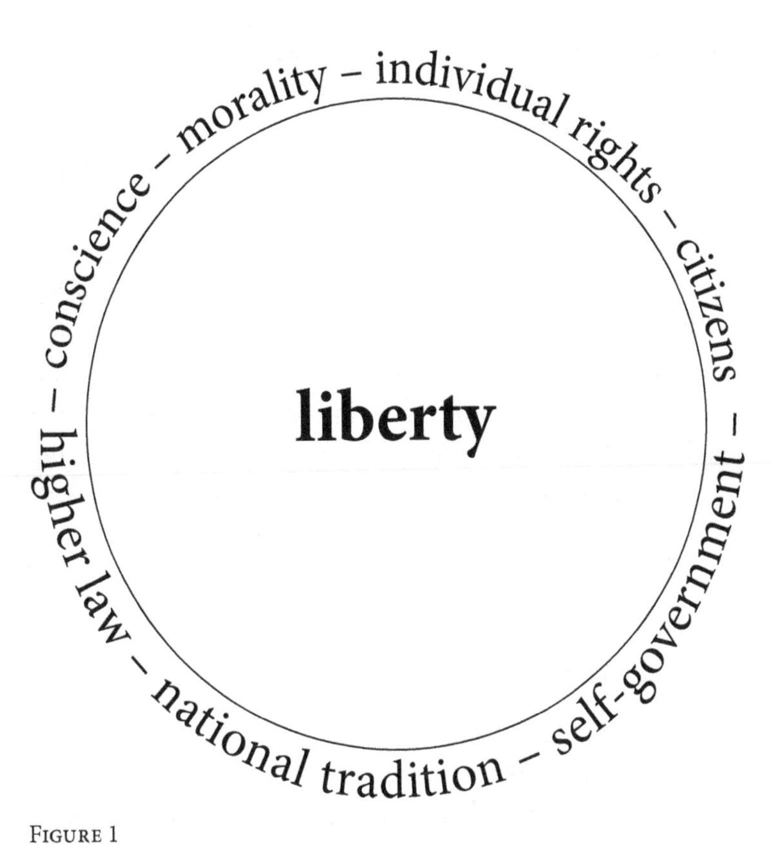

FIGURE 1
A diagram of Acton's theory of liberty

good, but by becoming better, not by its perfection but by its improvement." He rephrases this idea in his inaugural lecture at the University of Cambridge: "The wisdom of divine rule appears not in the perfection but in the improvement of the world; and that achieved liberty is the one ethical result that rests on the converging and combined conditions of advancing civilization."

Providence's work has an impact, directly or indirectly, on all the elements of liberty listed in the figure. It also ensures the supreme position of liberty in the world of political ideas. That is why liberty, in spite of being "beset by its natural enemies, by ignorance and superstition, by lust of conquest and by love of ease, by the strong man's craving for power, and the poor man's craving for food," cannot be annihilated. Its development can be "utterly arrested," even reversed, but, faced with hostile conditions, liberty takes on unexpected forms. Acton provides two examples of such paradoxical transformation, when freedom's ordinary foes turn into its last line of defense: first, corruption and, second, venality of offices. Conditions in Tsarist Russia illustrate the first because the proverbial bribery of tsarist magistrates in fact served as a relief from autocratic oppression. French provincial courts (*parlements*) are an example of the second because they morphed into the only legal opposition to the ancien régime.

Mature Liberty

In holding up liberty as the highest political idea, Acton emphasized that it is a process, not a state, that grew from small seeds planted in ancient Israel and continued for centuries in its immature forms until it reached the early stages of maturity in the late seventeenth and eighteenth centuries. "It is a delicate fruit of a mature civilisation." Taking a closer look at this development will allow us to pinpoint a set of values that are beyond the core principles in his theory but indispensable for mature forms of liberty and the emerging liberalism of the Actonian kind.

By the time of the Glorious Revolution (1688), England had a centuries-old national tradition with strong elements of freedom that could be traced back to the Magna Carta (1215). That tradition recognized the superiority of higher (natural) law, which it inherited from the Middle Ages, and the limitation of royal power, originally by great lords and increasingly by Parliament. In the seventeenth century, the country stubbornly resisted royal attempts at arbitrary power, ultimately ending in civil war and the deposition of the Stuart dynasty on two occasions (1649, 1688). The Glorious Revolution affirmed Parliament's superiority over the crown, the principle of representation—the people, however understood and defined, are the true sovereign represented by Parliament—and the separation of powers between the legislative branch, on the one hand, and the executive and judicial branches still held by the king, on the other. The Bill of Rights (1689), along with the Triennial Act (1694) and the Act of Settlement (1701), formally confirmed this arrangement and granted certain civil rights to Englishmen.

According to Acton, this was the beginning of mature liberty in England, with "liberty founded on inequality" at first but ending around the turn of the nineteenth century with the American notion of "liberty founded on equality." Initially, it had many imperfections, such as the denial of voting rights to the overwhelming majority of the English, an incomplete division of powers, domination of the royal court over Parliament through bribery, corruption of the electoral districts, especially through the so-called rotten boroughs, and so on. Still, the nation (or the people)—however small in terms of those who could vote—was recognized as the source of power and enjoyed the right of representation, thereby limiting royal government. As Acton claims, what counts is "the healthy development of liberty, not its present attainment."

Despite the weaknesses of its new order, England took a straight course leading it to a fully liberal regime by gradually spreading suffrage, completing the division of powers, introducing the executive branch based on parliamentary majority, guaranteeing freedom in economic activity, and ensuring civil rights, which were increasingly understood as "the rights of man," not just the rights of Englishmen. In this process insular English Whiggism took on a more universal form of liberalism, yet of the evolutionary kind that concurred with national tradition. It respected it instead of rejecting it.

A similar though more rapid process took place in the American colonies. Franchise was widespread, and therefore Americans built their "liberty founded on equality." As mentioned, the colonists enjoyed strong self-government and had no old laws or aristocracy that would hamper pragmatic changes in their colonial regimes. The American Revolution united the former colonies and created government that would not restrict civic and civil liberty for its white inhabitants, yet still remained strong. The Founding Fathers apparently learned from the Roman Republic that "power, when it is divided, need not be diminished."

Acton extolled all the divisions provided by the US Constitution: the ancient division by the number of people exercising power—the rule of one (the president), a few (the Senate), and the many (the House of Representatives); the modern tripartite division of powers; indirect presidential election, federalism, and the Supreme Court. Federalism aroused his particular enthusiasm because it is "the true natural check on absolute democracy . . . which limits the central government by the powers reserved, and the state governments by the power they have ceded. It is the one immortal tribute of America to political science, for state rights are at the same time the consummation and the guard of democracy."

When they were ultimately ratified by the states (1788–1791), the US Constitution and the Bill of Rights created a fully developed liberal order. Acton criticizes its various weaknesses and, with his characteristic penchant for hyperbole, calls it "a monstrous fraud," nonetheless redeemed by federalism. Subsequently, as in England, the new regime entered a quiet phase of evolution that would smooth its rough edges and advance its liberal character. This organic process was interrupted, however, because of two constitutional flaws that proved to be fatal and led to civil war: slavery and inadequately defined state rights. Acton condemned slavery, but he equally denounced the cost of abolishing it through "the most sanguinary civil war of modern times." He felt slavery should have been abrogated piecemeal; this would have been a natural way of progress for his organic, evolutionary liberalism.

But what he feared the most and what ultimately pushed him to support the Southern Confederacy was the growth of doctrinaire threads in American liberalism.

> All constitutional questions are referred to the one fundamental principle of popular sovereignty, without consideration of policy or expediency. . . . The same intolerance of restraints and obligations, the same aversion to recognize the existence of popular duty . . . disturb their notions of government and of freedom. The influence of these habits of abstract reasoning, to which we owe the revolution in Europe, is to make all things questions of principle and of abstract law. A principle is always appealed to in all cases, either of interest or necessity, and the consequence is that a false and arbitrary political system produces a false and arbitrary code of ethics, and the theory of abolition is as erroneous as the theory of freedom.

By pursuing abstract principles—equality and popular sovereignty—without regard for national tradition and expediency, America started down a perilous road that increased the power of the democratic agent in its government, subverted states' rights and civic liberty, and ultimately switched its affinity from evolutionary liberalism (or Anglo-American liberalism) to its doctrinaire (continental) kind. We may add that this process did not end in Acton's time but continues into our days.

The next layer in Acton's theory of liberty is the position of the working class and the poor. These are important ingredients in his theory as they reveal the fundamental difference between his liberalism and laissez-faireism—the dominant thread in nineteenth-century liberalism—and as they led to some branding him a socialist.

One of the canonical principles of the liberalism of those days was the belief that power should belong to property. Scared of the masses—uneducated and prone to following demagogues—liberals supported property requirements, even at the cost of excluding a great majority from voting rights and the betrayal of their cherished value, equality. Acton admits that he shared similar fears but ultimately changed his mind seeing a "monstrous" injustice in denying suffrage to the workers.

Looking at the situation in England, he lists several arguments against such an exclusion. First, the wealthy, as employers, exercise economic control over the working class. Property requirements, however, add another kind of control over labor, this time as legislators and holders of state power. "It cannot be right that one of the two contracting parties [employers] should have the making of the laws, the management of the conditions, the keeping of the peace, the administration of justice, the distribution of taxes, the control of expenditure, in its own hands exclusively." Second, if there is some justification for a claim that the working class is unfit to govern, the fact is that "every class is unfit to govern. . . . The upper class used to enjoy undivided say, and used it for their own advantage . . . by laws which were selfish and often inhuman." Third, Adam Smith (1723–1790) made labor the source of wealth. If this is so, then the workers cannot be excluded from power. They cannot hold power alone, as French revolutionaries and socialists maintained, but should share it with the propertied class. In conclusion, Acton observed in 1881 that the loss of "undivided power" by the upper class had already brought tangible benefits for the English masses and hoped that this process would continue. In this he reconfirms his strong beliefs in a natural growth and the ameliorating capacities of evolutionary, organic liberalism: "The law of liberty tends to abolish the reign of race over race, of faith over faith, of class over class."

The final feature of his theory is an emphasis on caring for the destitute and suffering. They cannot be excluded from participating in the advantages brought by civilization:

> Progress has imposed increasing sacrifices on society, on behalf of those who can make no return, . . . whose existence is a burden, an evil, eventually a peril to the community. The mean duration of life . . . is prolonged by all the chief agents of civilization . . . , and depends on preserving, at infinite cost . . . the crippled child and the victim of accident, the idiot and the madman, the pauper and the culprit, the old and infirm. . . . This growing dominion of disinterested motive, this liberality towards the weak in social life, corresponds to that respect for the minority in political life, which is the essence of freedom.

Acton's notion of liberty did not mean the free rein of either the strong and wealthy (a kind of vulgar liberalism that follows a doctrinaire, Hobbesian-like, laissez-faire approach to life) or the proletarian masses (a regime advocated by socialists and other radicals), but it excluded no one and gave to all what is due.

Organic, Evolutionary Liberalism versus Doctrinaire, Continental Liberalism

Acton's theory of liberty corresponds with the liberalism he professed, which we have termed as organic, evolutionary liberalism. He was, no doubt, an ardent liberal. In his own words, liberalism was like a religion to him, a religion of the good, the noble, and the just who have served the cause of liberty and civilization throughout human history, beginning in antiquity. Naturally, since his kind of liberalism has roots in Whiggism—it is Whiggism that initiates "mature liberty"—all earlier noble sprits were not exactly liberals, but liberals' predecessors, their forebearers: protoliberals, if you will.

Like his theory of liberty, Actonian liberalism puts liberty at the center—after all, the term is a derivative of the Latin *liber* (free) and *libertas* (liberty)—and has all the other characteristics enumerated earlier: first, the core principles in the diagram (figure 1) and then all auxiliary rules developed in the phase of mature liberty, most of which are shared with all shades of liberalism. To grasp more clearly the nature of Acton's liberalism, let us contrast it with the liberalism he denounced.

As said earlier, Acton did not tolerate arbitrary political principles, except the recognition of liberty as the supreme political ideal and rights as derived from natural law. Regimes are to grow as does a language or a tree, having a higher law and their political tradition as guides. This made him an odd liberal, for the liberal mainstream of his day rejected national tradition and increasingly appealed to abstract rules, seeking "scientific" foundations for political, social, and ethical order and for justifying the replacement of existing regimes. Initially, the liberal mainstream thought those foundations lay in the concept of state of nature that Thomas

Hobbes (1588–1679) invented, John Locke (1632–1704) liberalized, and French *philosophes* popularized. In Acton's own time, this concept took the form of utilitarianism.

The idea of state of nature gave rise to natural rights theory and the contractarian concept of state, society, and law. These theories perfectly fitted the needs of the nascent liberalism because they provided "rational" and "scientific" basis for the rights of man—what today we call civil rights—and constitutional law, as well as a yardstick for assessing existing polities. Self-preservation, liberty, and equality are the rights individuals have by nature, preceding any form of communal life and state foundation. That is, they are inborn and inalienable. Early modern thinkers differed as to other features of the state of nature—and consequently, what follows—but they all agreed that civil society and the state result from a (usually) voluntary contract.

The scientific claims for the natural rights theory were demolished by David Hume (1711–1776) and indirectly by Immanuel Kant. Subsequently, nineteenth-century liberalism fell under the spell of utilitarianism, originated by Jeremy Bentham (1748–1832) and completed by John Stuart Mill. Leaving aside other features of utilitarianism, what was the most important from the standpoint of political and social life was Bentham's formula of "the greatest happiness for the greatest number." That formula of "social utility" was to provide clear guidelines for legislation and morality, dispensing with voluntarism and doubts in political decisions as well as in social norms. What did Acton find wrong with those theories, and why did he criticize them so severely?

Acton viewed the concept of state of nature and theories derived from it as disastrous for liberty. They were intellectual constructs with no empirical basis. As such, they could be useful for the examination of "ascertained evils" in politics, but they could not "serve as a basis for reconstruction of civil society, [just] as medicine cannot serve for food."

The French Revolution illustrates this point well. Its leaders, whether liberal or radical, judged the ancien régime by the standards of state of nature. Those standards rendered the regime, together with its society of estates, as thoroughly unnatural and thus in need of total change by whatever means. To fit the doctrine, all institutions, laws, and traditions—in particular religion—had to be annihilated, corporate and provincial rights abolished, and any resistance crushed. Existing reality was to be trimmed according to prescribed norms. As a result, an absolute royal will was replaced by a much more powerful popular will, from which there was no higher court of appeal. At this point Acton agreed with Tocqueville that the Revolution did not reduce but multiplied the power of central government and, consequently, damaged the cause of liberty, even if the abolition of the ancien régime was its great merit.

The damage to liberty and liberalism also had a long-term dimension. The first constitution of the French Revolution—passed in its still liberal phase in September of 1791—was used throughout the nineteenth century as the model constitution by other European states in the process of liberalizing their regimes. They thus copied the French methods for dealing with reality, quelling all that stood in their way. In other words, parliamentary representatives of the sovereign (the people) were omnipotent in executing the popular will, yet the people themselves were reduced to pawns. By annihilating national tradition, particularly by demolishing all intermediary institutions, new regimes created a society of atomized individuals who exercised their citizenship once every few years, at the moment of voting. In this way, doctrinaire, constructivist liberalism granted the people civil rights and formal participation in power, yet at the cost of subverting civic liberty, that is, the citizenry acting through intermediary institutions and taking their affairs into their own hands.

As for the utilitarian version of liberalism, Acton's principal objection was to its substitution of social utility for liberty. To achieve desirable aims from the standpoint of social utility, the government must resort to social engineering, that is, favoring some by discriminating against others, and using coercion against resisters. Consequently, instead of being the supreme aim in politics, liberty became its first victim. This was certainly not the freedom he cherished or the liberalism he had in mind. On the contrary, he branded it, together with its older, eighteenth-century version, as illiberal distortion that tarnished the image of what he deemed "true" liberalism.

It is interesting that Acton did not mention another change in liberalism, essential to its development, of which a thinker of his erudition must have been aware. If we can search for the roots of liberalism deep in the past—sometimes even as far back as antiquity, but usually the Renaissance and/or the seventeenth century—the term itself did not exist until the first half of the nineteenth century. The classical liberal Adam Smith did not know it and used the term *liberal* as an adjective, being a derivative of *liberality* rather than *liberty*. Friedrich von Hayek links the origins of the word *liberal* as a noun and *liberalism* as a political term with the emergence of political parties, first in Spain (Liberales, 1812), then in France (Libéraux, 1818). In England, the term "liberal" gained popularity in the 1840s and 1850s with the amalgamation of the Whigs and the philosophical radicals, who eventually adopted a new name: the Liberal Party.

Nationalism, Democracy, State, and Society

To complete the picture of the Actonian theory of liberty and organic liberalism, let us briefly review his attitude toward nationalism, democracy, and the state and society.

Nationalism

In a seminal essay, "Nationality," Acton distinguishes between two kinds of nationalism: the first, which he calls "national liberty," is in fact a version of organic, Anglo-American liberalism; the second, "national unity," is an offshoot of doctrinaire liberalism.

National liberty can develop in multinational states if they respect the principles of organic liberalism. Special rights and/or autonomy for national minorities limit the central government, thereby serving as an impediment to its evolving into unlimited power. Acton views central government as a natural and benevolent institution, indispensable for the welfare of any polity but, like Tocqueville, he also sees it as one of the greatest threats to civic liberty. A tripartite division of powers is in itself an insufficient restraint on the elemental drift of national government into unlimited rule. The rights of national minorities strengthen the resistance against this drift and therefore help in maintaining a balanced government.

Acton finds other advantages to various nations living together in one state. First, their particular national rights—next to that of the Catholic Church—are the oldest check on central (royal) authority, going back to the Middle Ages. Second, relations among several nationalities play a role analogous to interaction among individuals: the more heterogenic the partners, the healthier their offspring. Likewise, nationalities entering into contact with others have a chance to imitate and adopt institutions, customs, and laws superior to their own. And third, nationalities whose tradition and autonomy are respected (who are not excluded from but included in the life of a multinational state) can develop into a new nation based on rights, not on ethnicity. Acton finds this "nationality" far superior to one based on the ethnic principle.

The second kind of nationalism—national unity—was a side effect of the French Revolution, the Napoleonic conquests, and the Congress of Vienna. The Revolution drew the masses into politics, originally in France and subsequently in the countries invaded by French armies. The slogan of the rights of man—confirmed later by the Napoleonic Code—was proclaimed wherever those armies went. Yet the commoners in Italy, Germany, and Spain quickly realized that their French liberators were more rapacious than their feudal lords on top of being alien. Some turned against the French to liberate their country; others dreamed about uniting themselves in one state. The Congress of Vienna (1815), however, completely ignored the national factor in its decisions. As a result, disappointed nationalities resorted to fighting either for national independence (in the multinational Austrian, Russian, and Ottoman Empires) or for unity in a single state (Italy and Germany). Thus was modern nationalism born, combining an emphasis on the national right to independence with a doctrinaire approach to achieving it.

The birth and evolution of nationalism are complex processes that will be further explained in the next chapter on the history of liberty. For our present purposes, it is sufficient to say that modern nationalism perverted the idea of national rights as doctrinaire liberalism twisted the idea of individual freedom. The right to live in one's own state evolved into the idea that the state and nation are coextensive, that the state by virtue of being national excludes from power other nationalities within its borders, and that the nation has the right to all territories inhabited by its members. Consequently, nationalism brings with it wars and enslavement because it delegitimizes most existing state borders, provokes conflicts among nationalities living in mixed settlements, and discriminates against national minorities. Ultimately, it enslaves the nation as such, both in one nation-state and in multinational states. In the former, it subjects individuals to the collective will and conscripts them into national service; in the latter, the dominant nation discriminates against national minorities but forfeits its own freedom, because it relies on an arbitrary government to keep those minorities in check.

Acton was critical of unlimited democracy, especially if it took the form of socialism. But his evaluation of nationalism was more severe. He called it "a retrograde step in history" that is "more absurd and more criminal than the theory of socialism." The renewed interest in Acton's thought prior to and after World War II certainly stems from such warnings.

Democracy

Acton's assaults on democracy can be found everywhere in his writings. Judging by the number of these attacks, one might think he was a hardcore antidemocrat. If so, then how can we explain his admiration for American democracy? And even more so, how can we explain his approval for the extension of voting rights and the abolition of slavery (he condemned not abolition itself but the method used)? This certainly made America more democratic. An even more striking example is his native England, whose political order at the end of the seventeenth century gave rise to mature liberty yet still kept old limitations on voting rights. Acton clearly preferred a more democratic American "liberty founded on equality" to the English undemocratic "liberty founded on inequality." Furthermore, he fully supported the evolution of English constitutionalism into a more inclusive system by granting the right to vote to an ever-growing number of the people. As mentioned, his evolutionary, organic liberalism has self-regulating and self-improving mechanisms, which make political order not less but more democratic.

There is no question that Acton's best practical regime, one that meets the standards of organic liberalism and national liberty, is a well-balanced democracy. But if this is so, how can we explain his hostile remarks on democracy?

The answer is twofold. First, he was not against democracy itself, that is, the core principles that make it up (popular sovereignty, legal equality, widespread franchise, and majority rule), but against arbitrary democracy in which those principles are unconstrained by other rules (higher constitutional law, the separation of powers, rights for minorities, and intermediary bodies). Second, he was deeply concerned about some inherent flaws of democracy that, if ignored and uncontrolled, turn into a dire threat to freedom. Let us now take a brief look at his views on both pure democracy and democracy's shortcomings.

Without a doubt, Acton abhorred pure, unlimited democracy. He mentioned many examples of such regimes throughout history, but none was so striking and (in)famous as Athenian democracy. He characterized it as the "tyranny of numbers," sometimes replacing "tyranny" with such terms as "oppression," "supremacy," or "sovereignty." Athens achieved this stage after the reforms of Pericles, particularly during the Peloponnesian War (431–404 BC). The popular assembly—the voice of the people—had the power to change any law by a simple majority, and its decisions were final, without the possibility of appeal. Furthermore, the assembly had the exclusive right to decide what was just and what was unjust. Becoming "the seat of knowledge of good and evil," it was at the same time "the seat of power." The combination of these two factors led the people to believe in their right to punish anyone, even those who had done nothing wrong, and they considered it "monstrous to prevent them from doing whatever they pleased." This amounted to collective despotism or, as Acton put it, the "people of Athens became a tyrant."

If the question of arbitrary power of the majority can be solved, or at least we have learned how to limit it, the second set of problems—democracy's intrinsic flaws—is more difficult to deal with and to remedy. Acton mainly lists four such problems.

First, he points out the essential difference between the evolution of arbitrary regimes based on the rule of one or a few and those based on the rule of the many. Government controlled by a minority (monarchy, aristocracy) gradually loses its oppressive character, while majority government (democracy) tends to increase its power and intolerance of resistance to it. "Liberty depends on the division of power. Democracy tends to unity of power." Why is that so? Acton explains it in the following way:

> Democracy tends naturally to realize its principle, the sovereignty of the people, and to remove all limits and conditions of its exercise; whilst monarchy tends to surround itself with such conditions. In one instance force yields to right; in the other might prevails over law. The resistance of the king is gradually overcome by those who resist and seek to share power; in democracy the power is already in the hands of those who seek to subvert and to abolish the law. . . . In a purely popular government this antagonism of forces does not exist, for all power is united in the same sovereign; . . . there is no external power that can enforce the surrender of a part of the supreme authority, or establish a security against its abuse. . . .

> Hence monarchy grows more free . . . , whilst democracy becomes more arbitrary. The people is induced less easily than the king to abdicate the plenitude of its power.

Second, he notices that the threat to a minority posed by a ruling majority is much more sinister than that of the ruling minority to the majority: "It is bad to be oppressed by a minority, but it is worse to be oppressed by a majority. For there is a reserve of latent power in the masses which . . . the minority can seldom resist. But from the absolute will of an entire people there is no appeal, no redemption, no refuge but treason." Tocqueville in *Democracy in America* and later John Stuart Mill in *On Liberty* made similar points on the overwhelming character of the tyranny of majority.

Third, as no other regime, democracy is prone to sudden changes of opinion, to sheep-like or mass-like behavior, and to a disregard for law, merit, decency, and, ultimately, truth and common good. These vices of democracy aroused his strongest condemnation and fear:

> Tocqueville, Calhoun, Mill . . . have showed democracy without respect for the past, or care for the future, regardless of public faith, and of national honour, extravagant and inconstant, jealous of talent and knowledge, indifferent to justice but servile towards opinion, incapable of organisation, impatient of authority, averse from obedience, hostile to religion and to established law. . . . Democracy . . . sacrifices everything to maintain itself, and strives, with an energy . . . that kings and nobles cannot attain, to override representation, to annul all forces of resistance . . . , and to secure . . . free play for the will of the majority. The . . . principle, that none shall have power over the people, is taken to mean that none shall be able to restrain or to elude its power. The . . . principle, that the people shall not be made to do what it does not like, is taken to mean that it shall never be required to tolerate what it does not like.

Finally, democracy often falls victim to electoral manipulations. This occurs when electoral districts are so large that the voters vote for candidates who are unknown to them, a common condition in the democracy of our time. Then "the election is not free. It is managed by wire-pullers, and by party machinery, beyond the control of the electors." Consequently, the parliamentary majority is not really the majority but only represents the party that through "force or fraud" won the election. If this was a cause for concern in Victorian Britain, is it not a cause for alarm in our own time, in which the art of voter manipulation has degenerated into merely a set of skills and tools for political victory?

Democratic vices, if unchecked, pose a grave threat to freedom. Federalism and other constraints put on the majority rule mitigate it, but they do not remove it, especially since our ability to remedy the listed democratic flaws is small. If, however, they are not checked and, worse, are combined with doctrinaire liberalism and omnipotent government, then that threat becomes deadly. This danger will be addressed in the next section.

State (Government) and Civic Society

The state postulated by Acton, one that meets the requirements of organic liberalism, recognizes liberty as its highest aim and treats all other goals (for example the previously cited "happiness, or prosperity, or power") as secondary, subordinate to the supreme end. That state is based on rights that all citizens have equally, irrespective of nationality and other distinguishing criteria. Its government is "for the accomplishment of public ends, altogether distinct from, and comparatively indifferent to, the special interest of any individual, or class, or element, such as religion or capital."

The Actonian state respects the rights of individuals not only in their personal sphere (as civil rights) but also in their communal, public dimension (as civic liberty). This means that it has no right to encroach into the area reserved for civic society and its intermediary institutions. "The power of the State is supreme only in its own sphere"; likewise, the family, the church, the municipality, universities, professional and business organizations, and other such bodies are supreme in their own sphere. As long as they operate according to their own character and within general law, the state bureaucracy has no right to interfere. Each is "protected by the State, none can be controlled by it."

"The state sets up a moral, objective law, and pursues a common object distinct from the ends and purposes of society." Civic society is, in turn, a living body, an arena for common actions and competing enterprises, and a place proper for the pursuit of the utilitarian aim of "the greatest happiness of the greatest number." To illustrate the role of the state toward society, Acton compares it to gloves that protect the hands or the skin that covers the body. If they both perform their functions well, each works for the benefit of the other.

Acton also uses another comparison to show the relationship between state and society. In the national liberty pattern, a multinational state has citizens that enjoy their rights as individuals and as members of various intermediary bodies, especially as national minorities, and gradually develop loyalty toward their state. This loyalty stems from respect for state law, increasingly gaining sanction on moral grounds, unlike loyalty based on the ethnic principle, which appeals to instincts and sentiments. This new political nation forms a spiritual community ("a soul"), protected by a political community ("a body"), that is, the state.

Acton's idea of the state is somewhat idealistic, a model of the best practical regime to be pursued. Political reality, however, does not usually accommodate this aim. "We often see it happen, that though society is an organism, the state is a mere machine; not fitted on to society like a glove, but rather compressing it like a thumb-screw; not growing out of society like its skin, but put upon it from without like a mould, into which society is forced to pour itself." Writing these words in 1861, Acton did not have in mind the Roman Empire or early modern absolute monarchy, but the new liberal regimes, established in nineteenth-century Europe, particularly in Italy. In their fight against the remnants of the old order, they used methods almost as brutal as those of the French Revolution and crushed all institutions that stood between the all-powerful government and the people. With noble aims, especially enforcing legal equality, they drastically increased the centralization of power at the cost of destroying civic society and getting atomized individuals as a side effect. Parliament as the principal safeguard of liberty proved worthless; even worse, it became itself an engine of the arbitrary state: "Under these circumstances representative institutions are a delusion and a snare, as they were in France from 1815 to 1848."

Implementing the policies of continental liberalism, the modern, centralized state displayed its capacity for annihilating civic liberty, its upholding of civil rights notwithstanding. Acton argued, however, that this danger can be much more menacing, if modern state and doctrinaire attitude, whether liberal or not, are combined with the forces of democracy. Why is that "mixture" so perilous?

The answer is relatively simple. All three share the propensity to centralize state power, use coercion in order to enforce the will of the people, pursue abstract ends (e.g., equality or happiness, or national interest), and disregard tradition and intermediary bodies. These predispositions are aggravated by specifically democratic vices listed in the previous section. As if that were not enough, Acton added one more: the democratic tendency to obliterate the distinction between state and society, and to use the former for the sake of latter.

> Pure democracy is that form of government in which the community is sovereign, in which, therefore, the State is most nearly identified with society. But society exists for the protection of interests; the State for the realization of right. . . . The State sets up a moral, objective law, and pursues a common object distinct from the ends and purposes of society. This is essentially repugnant to democracy, which recognizes only the interests and rights of the community. . . . There is no mediator between the part and the whole; there is no room, therefore, for differences of class, of wealth, of race; equality is necessary to the liberty which is sought by a pure democracy.

Acton speaks of pure democracy, but in light of what he says about democracy in general, no democracy can be free from this tendency. The problem diminishes proportionally to the constraints and counterbalances placed on democracy—as well as on the government—but it does not seem possible to completely eradicate it. The same could be said about other democratic vices: their impact can be constrained but not eliminated.

As a result, we could infer that Acton warns us about a variety of threats resulting from the combination of the modern state, the doctrinaire approach to reality, and democracy: two extremes and the spectrum of dangers between them. On one end we could place a predatory, Hobbesian-like regime that recognizes no limitations, seeks either radical equality or *Lebensraum*, promises a future bliss, and enjoys either a forced or genuine support of the masses. This kind of regime wreaked havoc in twentieth-century Europe; ex post, we named it "totalitarianism." Acton did not know this term, but his warnings about the impending danger were so vivid and striking that the generations who endured World War II and those who succeeded them had no problem in reading those warnings. That is why they considered him as one of their contemporaries and treated him as their prophet.

On the other end we could place a regime that Tocqueville called a "soft despotism" (Acton was not so precise). Such a regime is not predatory but protective; it seeks equality and happiness. To achieve them, it takes care of the people by providing for their security, needs, pleasures, and work, and, finally, as Tocqueville expressed it, spares them "the trouble of thinking and all the pain of living." The price for this luxury is, however, civic self-reliance, independence, and, ultimately, freedom. If the previous nightmare came through the agency of communism and National Socialism, its soft counterpart is a child of utilitarianism, but both are byproducts of the modern state, a doctrinaire stance, and an insufficiently constrained mass democracy. Acton issued the following warning for posterity that seems to include both hardcore and softcore nightmares: "State absolutism, not royal absolutism, is the modern danger against which neither representative government nor democracy can defend us, and which revolution greatly aggravates. If we do not bear this in mind, we shall be led constantly astray by forms to overlook the substance, to confound freedom of speech with freedom of action, to think that right is safer against majorities than against tyrants, that liberty is permanently safer in Belgium, Piedmont, or the United States, than in France, Russia, or Naples."

When we put together Acton's scattered remarks on freedom, conscience, self-government, mature liberty, and liberalism—the kind he preferred as well as the kind he renounced—they can form a remarkably coherent theory of liberty. Recognizing freedom as the end of government, that theory consists of two essential parts: first, a set of core principles such as higher law, self-governance, morality, national tradition and its organic growth, and citizens and their rights; and, second, corollary rules and policies complementing the former and making freedom mature. This set includes, inter alia, representative government, majority rule, separation of powers, other methods of dividing and mixing government, widespread suffrage, respect for intermediary institutions, and care for the needy. Together they form what Acton calls mature liberty, which can be also termed ordered liberty.

Despite additional remarks on the state, society, democracy, and good and bad regimes, his theory of liberty suffers from generality, lacking the structural details characteristic of other liberal theories. It does not, however, need those details, because it creates a regime that triggers built-in mechanisms of self-regulation and self-improvement. They act as if they were the *invisible hand* in the politics of liberty. Where other theories need meticulous management and control, and resort to social engineering to achieved predesigned aims, his order evolves by a process of natural growth and development. That is why the Actonian theory of liberty brings to life a liberal order that can be called organic and evolutionary, while its counterpart is doctrinaire and constructivist and is therefore ultimately not liberal but illiberal.

His theory also has another remarkable feature: the absence of intrinsic conflicts between the individual and society. What remains a permanent conundrum for the doctrinaire liberals on how to reconcile the individual and the community does not exist in Acton's postulated order. In his theory, men and women are not egotistical individuals, caring mainly for themselves and doomed to confrontation with others as well as with the order in which they live, but moral beings who are active citizens and who participate in shaping their community.

Acton's theory includes a sober assessment of the modern state. In this, he is not alone among the nineteenth-century liberals. However, his criticism of the modern state does not stem from a view of government as a necessary evil and the laissez-faire corollary "that government is best which governs least." No, like Tocqueville, he considered it an essential good, yet dangerous for liberty if unchecked and unbalanced, and without active and well-organized citizens operating through strong local governments.

The same can be said about democracy. Acton maintained that political power originates in the people and that the advancement of civilization leads to the recognition of legal equality, ever-wider suffrage, and representative government. Consequently, the natural form of rule in the modern world is a kind of democracy, although one limited and constrained in more rigorous and complex manners than other regimes. His concept of organic liberalism and national liberty give us a glimpse of his best practical regime. It is a well-balanced democracy that recognizes liberty as its supreme aim; has active citizens running their own affairs through local self-governments of different levels and through intermediate institutions; respects national tradition while allowing for its organic growth; divides and balances national government in all possible ways; recognizes the distinction between state and society; and treats its citizens equally, irrespective of their nationality (therefore also of race and gender, to extend this approach to our time), thus ensuring their individual rights.

Like Tocqueville, however, Acton sensed the democratic problem. Tocqueville posed the alternative to democracy in freedom and democracy in soft despotism. Acton was far more pessimistic.

Democracy has inherent tendencies for arbitrary power; total control over minorities and individuals; intolerance of any nonconformism; sudden changes in moods and opinions; and disrespect for established laws, institutions, merit, and national tradition. It is also susceptible to manipulation by powerful interest groups that pretend to express the will of the majority. Democracy, therefore, requires constant vigilance, for otherwise it can morph imperceptibly into ever-changing forms of oppression, from "softcore" abuses to Orwellian-like totalitarianism, and other forms of tyranny in between.

Democracy cannot change its nature and we ought to remember that it is a means to an end, not an end in itself. Rather than worshipping it without reservation, we must keep in mind its potential to be the worst as well as the best of regimes.

3

Acton's History of Liberty

During the 1870s and early 1880s, Acton thought about writing a history of liberty. As mentioned in chapter 1, this plan gradually turned into the "Madonna of the Future." This was due mainly to the very high self-imposed scholarly standards he set for this project, adherence to an increasingly unpopular idea of treating history as a moral tribunal, and problems in his personal life. The book thus remained "the greatest book that never was written." What was left of this great project was two lectures delivered to the members of the Bridgnorth Institution in February and May 1877, published as "The History of Freedom in Antiquity" and "The History of Liberty in Christianity," a lengthy review of Erskine May's *Democracy in Europe* (1878), and plenty of notes on this topic, now kept at the Cambridge University Library. Additionally, he left many scattered remarks on liberty that can be found throughout his writings but especially in two collections of his Cambridge lectures, published as *Lectures on Modern History* (1906) and *Lectures on the French Revolution* (1910), his essay on "Nationality" (1862), "Political Causes of the American Revolution" (1861), and a series of articles and notes on the ongoing process of Italian unification.

Unlike other liberals, Acton did not seek freedom in the primeval past (state of nature) or derive from it inalienable "rights of man." He did not appreciate the utilitarian principle of social utility either. His notion of freedom was the political liberty of committed individuals who build and maintain political communities. In other words, he meant civic liberty, in which citizens run public affairs and are free in their decision-making, limited only by natural law. Such political communities of active and morally motivated citizens aiming at liberty do not emerge suddenly. On the contrary, they grow step by step, require arduous efforts and vigilance, and often experience setbacks and retreats. They seem to never appear in perfect form—even Acton's best practical regime remains a signpost—but, with the exception of the age of absolute monarchy, which denied people's sovereignty outright, they never completely disappear in Western civilization either. In previous chapters we touched upon important points from Acton's history of liberty. It is now time to present it in more detail.

The Origins and Foundations of Civic Liberty

Ancient Israel

Acton sees the first signs of civic liberty in ancient Israel. In chapter 2 we described the Hebrew notion of freedom and the circumstances in which it arose. To this we add three points that he emphasized as crucial to the birth of this concept of liberty. First, the Israelites had no central authority between their arrival in the Promised Land and the beginning of their monarchy (1047 BC). For nearly three centuries, they lived under a "voluntary covenant" of tribes and clans, united by common ancestors and religion but separated by full autonomy in the conduct of their own affairs. This established their national political tradition, which continued under monarchy. Second, royal authority was limited by divine law, the same for the rulers and the subjects. And, third, whenever the king broke the law, the prophets dared to point this out and demanded his repentance. All of this met the criteria Acton believed indispensable to political liberty: national tradition and its organic growth, and a higher law independent of human will.

The Jewish chapter in the history of liberty ended abruptly with the Babylonian Captivity (586 BC), though not without an impact on posterity. In the seventeenth century, Protestant sects resorted to the Jewish pattern of rule as a means of defense against persecution by church authorities—both Catholic and Protestant—and by absolute monarchs.

Ancient Greece

About the time freedom suffered setbacks in Israel, it found a new and hospitable place in Greece, taking Athens as its new home. Ancient Greece invented and spread throughout the Mediterranean space (including the Black Sea) an original form of regime, the *polis* (plural: *poleis*). Usually referred to as a city-state, it was a community of citizens, equal—at least in theory—and participating in the government. Although most of the *poleis* had an oligarchic form of rule, run by a wealthy (or well-born) few, the many (*demos*) were not stripped of citizenship even if they were deprived of power.

The migration of liberty to Athens coincided with the reforms of the Athenian regime designed by Solon (594 BC). One of the Greek Seven Sages, Solon reversed the policies of previous lawgivers, in particular Archon Draco, consequently, "government by consent superseded government by compulsion." The poor still could not hold office but gained access to the popular assembly and courts. They therefore participated in electing officials and judging their conduct in case of abuse. The well-born (landowners) ruled but served without pay in the army; moreover, as citizen-soldiers, they had to arm themselves at their own expense. Solon's idea of government was that power is commensurate with service to the community. Acton points to this as the beginning of a limited democracy in Athens.

The disadvantageous position of the many in Athens changed after the victory of the Greeks over the Persian Empire (480 BC). The predominantly Athenian fleet routed its enemies' ships and so saved Greece's independence. The poor served as crews on Athenian ships, which is why they soon obtained all political rights. At the same time, Athens quickly became a sea power and maintained a large fleet.

Admitting the many to power did not provoke Acton's protests, yet he strongly objected to the sequel: the rapid descent of the Athenian regime from limited to unlimited democracy (by the end of the fifth century). As mentioned in chapter 2, the popular assembly could pass any law by a simple majority, increasingly displaying its penchant for arbitrary power and making often foolish decisions from which there was neither appeal nor escape. This was the regime that Acton so frequently called the tyranny (or sovereignty) of numbers and which he blamed for the Athenian Empire's collapse and for the unprecedented speed at which it occurred.

The Greek *poleis* gave rise to the idea that power comes from the people—more specifically, the citizens—who thus also assumed civic activity. In ancient Greece, citizenship was regarded as a great privilege and jealously guarded. Whoever did not take advantage of it and shunned the responsibilities that fell to the *polites* (citizen) was an *idiotes* (a private person, who did not grow up to be a citizen and remained uninterested in public life). In some respects, this attitude honored Acton's ideal of civic liberty. The Greek city-states, however, and particularly the Athenian *polis*, suffered from two pernicious flaws that prevented them from attaining mature freedom: first, they did not recognize a higher law, independent of human will; and, second, they did not have a notion of individual rights (such an idea was unheard of in antiquity); on the contrary, they maintained the crushing power of the community over the individual. As Acton says, "What the slave was in the hand of his master, the citizen was in the hands of the community." The *politai* (citizens) enjoyed many liberties, especially compared to the *metoikoi* or metics (resident aliens), but had no rights as individuals, much less a right to privacy.

If Greek political life provoked Acton's reservations, he admired their political thought. As in so many other fields, the Greeks initiated it and quickly took it to the greatest heights. Although in this process they committed "nearly all the errors that are undermining political society," they also unearthed treasures of political knowledge. They were painfully aware of "the right of the people to govern, and their inability to govern alone." The greatest of them, Plato and Aristotle, advocated mixed regimes (the rule of the one, of a few, and of the many), but Acton was skeptical about this solution. Such a regime never worked in practice, in particular as a means to limit democracy. To do so, it required additional constraints that were invented only in early modern times. Furthermore, he posited that the greatest Greek minds searched for an "intelligent government" that would "make men prosperous and happy" but ignored liberty. As mentioned, his attitude toward efficient and intelligent government was not favorable, as his strongly negative evaluation of early modern monarchy, in particular Machiavellian politics, revealed. He preferred that citizens, limited by a higher law, exercise power, even if their rule was not particularly good and intelligent.

Ancient Rome and Early Christianity

The long epoch of Rome, from the early republic to the late empire (roughly a thousand years), received a mixed evaluation from Acton. On the one hand, the Roman Republic was a ruthless oligarchy, remaining an ideal mixed regime only in the minds of the Greek historian Polybius and his followers, while the empire was an "odious despotism." On the other, he makes up a fairly long list of positive aspects of imperial rule to prove that it fared better in terms of freedom than the republic. First, imperial Rome kept communities of a *polis* type in its eastern provinces and contributed to their extension to its western part. They functioned as local self-governments, making Rome "a vast confederation of municipal republics." Civic spirit was thus preserved, even if limited to local affairs. Second, imperial Rome also spread Greek culture to the West and its own jurisprudence throughout the empire. Acton always maintained that civilization runs parallel to liberty; therefore, he counts this as Rome's merit. Third, the empire administered its provinces in much better ways, abolishing the worst abuses common in the republican period. Fourth, it legally mitigated slavery and generously granted citizenship to others, eventually giving it to all free men (AD 210). Fifth, the emperor's power was not a usurpation, at least formally, because it had democratic sanction. Grateful to Octavian Augustus for the end of civil wars and bloodshed, the Romans transferred their sovereign power to the emperor. In turn, the absolute nature of that power originated in the absolute power of the Roman people over the provinces of the empire.

The Roman Empire's merits notwithstanding, it was nevertheless a dead-end as far as freedom is concerned. A good illustration of this observation is the relationship between Christianity and its church and the ancient state.

Persecuted for about 250 years, Christians stubbornly defended their church's independence and defied the Roman state by excluding it from the religious sphere. They claimed that individuals have full autonomy in their relationship with God—in other words, freedom of conscience—and that the state may not intrude into it. The ancient state, however, was, in Acton's words, a "Church and State in one" or "two States in one." Religion was not a private or autonomous matter but stood at the center of politics. Ancient polity comprised citizens who were similar, in particular in their faith, severely punishing religious dissent (take the fate of Socrates, for example) and never admitting people of different cults to citizenship. The Romans resolved this problem better than the Greeks by recognizing alien gods as their own. What they demanded in return from the inhabitants of the multiethnic and multireligious empire was the worship of Rome and Augustus, that is, two gods that symbolized the empire and its ruler. This declaration of loyalty to the state worked well for polytheistic cults but not for believers in the one God. Originally, Christians enjoyed toleration as a Judaic sect, but with the deepening of the split between Judaism and Christianity they became a convenient scapegoat for Nero's madness. Beginning in AD 64, Christians became the victims of recurrent persecution that lasted until AD 313.

As much as it could, the early church tried to stay out of the public eye and taught obedience to the state. As mentioned, however, this docility had its limits. Based on Jesus's saying, "Render unto

Caesar the things that are Caesar's and unto God the things that are God's" (Matthew 22:21; Mark 12:17), the church did not allow the state to interfere in the relationship of the faithful with God and was ready to defend it even at the cost of martyrdom. Acton admired this heroic period of ancient Christianity, seeing resistance against state despotism as a fundamental mission of the church throughout history. That mission coincided with the interest of liberty—"Religion was the mother of freedom . . . freedom was the lawful offspring of religion"—and this was one of the reasons behind Acton's early apologetics for Christianity. His attitude changed, however, when he noticed that the church began to work in unison with the state after AD 313, and especially when he observed that it was the ancient state that prevailed and kept changing the church, rather than the other way around. "Even in the fervent age of its conversion the Empire employed its refined civilisation, the accumulated wisdom of ancient sages, the reasonableness and subtlety of Roman law, and the entire inheritance of the Jewish, the Pagan, and the Christian world, to make the Church serve as a gilded crutch of absolutism."

Despite lamenting the collapse of civilization that accompanied the fall of the Western Roman Empire, Acton concluded that this was a positive development for liberty. Without it, the future West would have followed the Eastern Roman Empire's pattern of organic evolution. Although of incomparably higher culture, the Byzantine civilization subjugated the church to the state, making it a mere branch of civil government, and produced a despotism that persisted "from the first to the last of Constantines." That tradition outlasted even the fall of Constantinople in 1453: adopted earlier by the Moscow principality, it continues throughout Russian history.

The Middle Ages: Liberty in the Society of Estates

The Eastern Empire retained ancient Roman knowledge, science, literature, arts, and skills. By contrast, the emerging West, suffering from Teutonic invasions and devastation, was moved far back "to a condition scarcely more advanced than that from which the institutions of Solon had rescued Athens." In the former, "even the peasants of Bulgaria knew the *New Testament* by heart" (which is another way of saying that literacy was widespread), while in the latter there was hardly a ruler who could write his own name. Byzantium, however, maintained not only the Roman level of civilization but the despotic regime as well. Its political tradition so drastically contradicted liberty that its organic growth could not produce anything but enslavement. Consequently, it was the ruined and backward West, not the sophisticated East, that could become a haven for freedom. And, as it turned out, it did. Although originally it could provide nothing more than a mere shelter, over time it offered liberty increasingly better conditions for growth and flourishing, becoming its home in the ages to come.

In listing the reasons for this development, Acton mentions three fundamental changes that took place in the Middle Ages: (1) the weakening of central government, (2) feudal fragmentation, and (3) the growing power of the church, which aroused his greatest interest. Let us review them briefly.

Medieval Government and Feudal Fragmentation

As regards the weak royal power of medieval rulers, it resulted from a variety of causes. The first and foremost is self-evident, and so Acton barely touches it: the Germanic conquerors did not have the sophistication, financial resources, and bureaucracy of the conquered. Roman administration was built up over centuries and, considering its simple means of communication (messengers traveling thousands of miles on horseback), was one of the marvels of antiquity. Although costly, it made possible the management of the vast empire. Once destroyed, it could not have been easily recreated, even by a talented and mighty ruler (such as Charlemagne in the early ninth century). This was achieved only in the fifteenth and sixteenth centuries with the emergence of the early modern nation-state. Second, the power of Germanic tribal chieftains was different from that of Roman emperors. Although chieftains held the power of the military commanders during war, in peacetime they depended on the decisions of their fellow tribesmen-warriors. They could be dangerous and cruel, but their power was weak. Third, with limited means, the rulers of new Teutonic kingdoms were incapable of controlling distant territories. The latter became the domain of local lords whose dependence on central government was conditional.

What originally appeared spontaneously—that is, the seizure of power by regional strongmen in the face of a power vacuum and the need for defense against marauding warriors (protection that the locals paid for with their independence)—gradually took on the legal form of a contract between the ruler and great lords. In the post-Charlemagne period, this developed into complex feudal arrangements, often called the feudal pyramid or ladder, with the king at the top, great lords just below, and knights of various ranks at the bottom of the privileged estate. In each case, two parties entered a contract in which the vassal pledged allegiance and service to the lord in exchange for the lord's protection and a fief (land estate). Additionally, the grand vassals maintained some administrative, judicial, and military functions and obtained immunity from royal interference. As a military class, all vassals benefited from state tax exemptions. Finally, a later rule that developed in the High Middle Ages (roughly 1050–1300) stated that "the vassal of my vassal is not my vassal" (England avoided this formula and all vassals were obliged to obey the king). All of this turned the feudal ladder into feudal chess in which each field (province/land) lived under the rule of a great lord who had his vassal-knights at his side. Acton captures this by quoting a French maxim that "every baron . . . is sovereign in his own domain." Further, each such a domain had separate statutes and laws and enjoyed different rights and obligations. The state thus became a conglomerate of provinces and lands that were loosely connected with the king and even less so with each other. Describing the essence of feudal relations—that is, vassalage—a modern scholar uses the following comparisons: "In this feudal arrangement there was an aspect of mutuality, of voluntary performance, and of implied contract which has almost wholly vanished from modern political relationships. It was somewhat as if a citizen might refuse to pay taxes beyond a certain amount, decline military service beyond a stipulated period, or perhaps refuse both until his liberties were recognized. In this respect the position of the king was weak in theory and often doubly weak in practice, and the feudal monarchy appears by comparison with a modern state to be highly decentralized."

Medieval fragmentation also had another dimension. Nearly all medieval states ignored ethnic borders, were multinational, and developed state loyalty—or state nationality akin to that mentioned in the previous chapter—only within a small elite, mainly the nobles. Common people had a local self-identity linked to a village, land, and faith but not the state in which they lived. The process of acquiring larger state and/or national identity was slow among them and took a rapid turn only after the outbreak of the French Revolution. Until then, popular sovereignty remained at the level of the privileged estates and the elite group of the commoners.

Medieval Church

As mentioned, in the process of an emerging post-Roman West, Acton was mainly interested in the growth of the church's position and role as a counterbalance to state government. He stresses that this situation was originally not a predesigned scheme on the part of the papacy and church hierarchy but a slow, organic development that offered the church opportunities as well as threats. Let us first take a look at the opportunities and then review the threats.

The ancient church dreaded the Roman Empire yet could not imagine its own existence outside of it. As it turned out, however, the fall of Rome brought the Western church and Christianity enormous gains. First, the Germanic winners converted to Christianity with relative ease. Although some of them passed first through Arianism (which the Council of Nicaea condemned as a heresy in AD 325), their opposition to Christianity was not as intransigent as in the Persian Empire and elsewhere. Second, the position of the church vis-à-vis the state was now reversed: it was the state that was disorganized, weak, and in need of help and the church that retained its structure (the network of dioceses and parishes) and staff and could offer help. The state had shrunk while the church seemed to grow. Third, since only the clergymen maintained some level of ancient education and skills, they quickly acquired a dominant position in the royal chancellery and a monopoly on education and obtained such privileges as tax exemption and their own courts.

As a result of these conditions, the church substantially increased its power and gained unprecedented opportunities to change the medieval state and society. Although politically divided, Europe preserved unity in the religious dimension and to a large extent in the legal, institutional, and cultural spheres. Developing first on Carolingian territories, these conditions gradually spread to the west, north, and east, extending to new nations and lands that joined the *respublica Christiana* (Christian Commonwealth): "The barbarians introduced . . . a single system of law, and thus became the instrument of a universal Church. The same spirit of freedom, the same notion of the State, pervade all the *Leges Barbarorum*, and all the polities they founded. . . . They differ . . . in almost all external things [but the] principle common to them all is to acknowledge the freedom of the Church as a corporation and a proprietor, and in virtue of the principle of self-government to allow religion to develop her influence in the State."

As for the threats that the church encountered in the new medieval conditions, they came originally from the Byzantine power and the brutality of the new Germanic masters and, as of the ninth century, from feudal arrangements and the ensuing struggle over the investiture of the clergy. As for the original threats, the Eastern Empire exercised control over a large (though dwindling) part of Italy until the late eighth century. The treatment of the bishop of Rome by the imperial government was no different from that of the eastern patriarchs, sometimes appointing or deposing popes. The Byzantine protection against the Lombards—the Germanic tribe that was increasingly spreading its domination over Italy—was illusory, and the papacy had to rely on its own efforts until it found a new protector, the Holy Roman Empire founded by Charlemagne in 800.

Subsequent weakening of the new empire made the papacy a victim of internal feuds among the Roman aristocracy, which selected and ousted popes the way Byzantine emperors used to. At the same time, the growth of feudalism threatened the papacy with the loss of control over the church and the church itself with its splintering into national churches and turning it into a pawn of civil power. Taking advantage of the feudal homage ceremony (land given to a vassal in exchange for his service and a pledge of fealty), in the tenth century the emperor began to appoint bishops and abbots of great monasteries. The ring and staff presented to clerical vassals, both symbolizing the passage of power over the benefices they received, implied that the emperor passed on spiritual power as well. Other European rulers soon followed suit.

The church responded to this development only in the eleventh century, at a time of growing assertiveness of popes and the church in general, which was then in the process of getting rid of "kings and wives," that is, regaining church independence and introducing celibacy. The protracted struggle between the papacy and the empire and, more broadly, between church and state, resulted in a compromise that was achieved in 1122. On the basis of the Concordat of Worms, the pope was to appoint high clergymen and the emperor was to secure a benefice (land), but the conflict, though reduced, continued and increasingly turned into a battle of ideas. Both sides sought the support of the people (invariably in medieval conditions this meant mainly the nobles) and gradually came to acknowledge the following principles: power comes from the people (the nation); the government ought to have the consent of the ruled and be limited; the law is superior to the will of the ruler; taxes require representation; and the people have the right to armed resistance in case of a breach of fundamental laws.

Acton summarized the result of the conflict between the church and state in the following words:

> To that conflict of four hundred years, we owe the rise of civil liberties. If the Church had continued to buttress the thrones of the kings whom it anointed, or if the struggle had terminated speedily in an undivided victory, all Europe would have sunk down under Byzantine or Muscovite despotism. For the aim of both contending parties was absolute authority. But although liberty was not the end for which they strove, it was the means by which the temporal and the spiritual power called the nations to their aid. The towns of Italy and Germany won their franchises, France got her States-General and England her Parliament out of the alternate phases of the contest; and as long as it lasted it prevented the rise of divine right.

Quoting the political teachings of St. Thomas (a supporter of the church), Acton judges that his language "contains the earliest exposition of the Whig theory." In turn, his opponent Marsilius of Padua (d. 1342) "saw in some respects farther than Locke or Montesquieu," though he lived about four hundred years earlier. In general, Acton admires the political produce of the Middle Ages:

> Representative government, which was unknown to the ancients, was almost universal. The methods of election were crude; but the principle that no tax was lawful that was not granted by the class that paid it—that is, that taxation was inseparable from representation—was recognised, not as the privilege of certain countries, but as the right of all. Not a prince in the world . . . can levy a penny without the consent of the people. Slavery was almost everywhere extinct; and absolute power was deemed more intolerant and more criminal than slavery. The right of insurrection was not only admitted but defined, as a duty sanctioned by religion. Even the principles of the *Habeas Corpus Act*, and the method of the Income Tax, were already known. The issue of ancient politics

was an absolute state planted on slavery. The political produce of the Middle Ages was a system of states in which authority was restricted by the representation of powerful classes, by privileged associations, and by the acknowledgment of duties superior to those which are imposed by man.

Early Modern (Nation) State and Absolutism versus Liberty

The Middle Ages entered their declining phase in the fifteenth century. The next century began a new epoch that lasted until the outbreak of the French Revolution (1789). The end of one epoch and the beginning of a new age are always the result of fundamental changes. In this instance, Acton identifies those changes as the Renaissance, geographic discoveries, Machiavelli's teachings, the Reformation, and the Scientific Revolution and calls them "violent shocks." After the shocks, there followed aftershocks: the Counter-Reformation, religious wars, and absolute monarchy. Acton seems to have an ambivalent attitude toward most of the shocks and definitely a negative view of the aftershocks, but he regards all of them as disastrous to liberty. Let us glance at his view of each.

As much as he appreciated the progress of liberty in the Middle Ages, he also saw its weaknesses, especially in areas that were vital to liberty or precious to him, such as knowledge. He charged the Middle Ages with being careless about facts, operating in "a twilight of fiction," and succumbing to passivity and a gloomy outlook on life. By contrast, the new age was restless, dynamic, rushing to "untried experience," optimistic, and thirsty for facts and a new and verifiable knowledge. This was what he liked about the Renaissance, geographic discoveries, and the Scientific Revolution. This was also the facet of the Reformation that he accepted, in particular its early emphasis on religious freedom and the struggle of the Protestant sects for their freedom of worship. The new age, however, scorned and abandoned its medieval heritage with respect to freedom and initiated dangerous, even lethal, ideas and policies that threatened liberty at its core (see figure 1 in chapter 2).

In addition to a new approach toward life, scholarly curiosity, and research, as well as great art and architecture, the Renaissance aggravated the corruption of the church, the papacy in particular, that had been evident as early as the late Middle Ages. The church increasingly ceased to counterbalance civil authority and thus to be a mainstay of freedom, but, under the influence of papal policies, it gradually became one of the major actors of politics, striving for supremacy over all states and rulers. In this strife, the papacy displayed greed and cynicism, used fraud and treachery, and even approved the murder of its enemies, thereby turning itself and the church in general into a caricature of itself, an edifice of monstrosity, a "fiend skulking behind the Crucifix." As it represented a spiritual power, operating "near the Conscience," this caused much graver harm to society than similar conduct by secular rulers. This is because "the spiritual danger of perverted morals is greater than the evil of perverted politics. It is an agency constantly active, pervading life, penetrating the soul" and poisoning what is the noblest in us. In the light of these words, we can better understand Acton's frustration with the Catholic Church and his intense contempt for its ethical failures.

Geographic discoveries resulted not only in finding new lands, growing commerce, and opportunities for social mobility but also in the revival of slavery, contempt for non-Christians, and brutal exploitation in Africa and Asia. The Scientific Revolution, in turn, always close to Acton's heart, opened a conflict between science and the teachings of the church and gave rise to doctrinaire liberalism. (Both issues were presented in chapters 1 and 2.) Suffice it to say that he dismissed the former and strongly condemned the latter. There is only one truth; therefore, misunderstanding and prejudice are at the root of the conflict between science and faith, a conflict that will eventually end in reconciliation.

Machiavellianism was repugnant to Acton (even if he had a few kind words for its author's scholarly methodology). First, it contradicted his view of history as a moral tribunal. Second, Machiavelli not only openly praised deception, disloyalty, murder, and cruelty but, worse, he treated them as expedient political necessities. In fact, he made them the essence of politics. According to Machiavelli, the prince (his generic term for a ruler) must engage in these activities if he is to succeed. Morality in politics does not exist, since politics aims at power, first to acquire and hold it and then to multiply it. Religious commandments and morality are to be kept only in private life; in politics, the prince must be ready to use any method without idly burdening his conscience. Power is paramount in politics; it is like a deity, and the prince must revere it as if he were its priest. The people are, therefore, nothing but a sacrifice offered on the altar of this ruthless deity.

Machiavelli's teachings were essential to the growth of royal power in the early modern period. His little book *The Prince* (first published in 1532) found avid readers among the European ruling elite and warped the consciences of otherwise righteous monarchs. By justifying political crimes, this work absolved the perpetrators and put the state above the law. It contributed considerably to the growth of the modern state and absolutism, which, as in antiquity, became "the greatest force on earth, bound by no code, a law to itself. As there is no such thing as right, politics are an affair of might, a mere struggle for power."

Whatever the faults of the Catholic Church, the papacy in particular, the Reformation did not serve the cause of freedom as the

English of Acton's time thought and as Protestants in general tend to believe. On the contrary, it opened a new chapter in the history of European despotism and paved the way for absolute monarchy. After an initial hesitation about religious freedom, Luther subordinated the church to the state, which eventually led to the acceptance of the principle *cuius regio eius religio* (in a prince's country, the prince's religion): "The result was a despotism such as the world had never seen. It was worse than the Byzantine system; for there no attempt was made to change the faith of the people. The Protestant princes exercised an ecclesiastical authority more arbitrary than the Pope had ever possessed; for the papal authority can only be used to maintain an existing doctrine, whilst theirs was aggressive and wholly unlimited. Possessing the power to command, and to alter in religion, they naturally acquired by degrees a corresponding absolutism in the civil order."

The church—both Protestant and Catholic—lost a chance to resume its natural mission vis-à-vis the state. Religious wars of the sixteenth and seventeenth centuries and the Catholic Reformation (or Counter-Reformation) only aggravated this problem. After subordinating the church as well as the nobles, the state drifted toward unlimited royal power, which ultimately ended in absolute monarchy. Acton emphasizes that this regime went further in the pursuit of uncontrolled power than any of its predecessors since Greek antiquity: it openly denied the principle of the people's sovereignty—something even Machiavelli had not done—and claimed it exclusively for itself.

Pursuing the Machiavellian idea of an efficient and intelligent government, absolute monarchs attempted to run their countries independently of estates assemblies and to break urban and provincial self-government and crush whatever was left of the former power of the privileged estates. In their place, they appointed officials, whom Acton contemptuously calls "legists, jurists, [and] bureaucrats." The system had to "proceed downward," managed by "experts" according to their procedures and rules. Eventually, this supposedly intelligent government brought misery for the people instead of prosperity, while the rulers, freed from moral constraints, made crime a matter of state policy. Consequently, the "isolated acts of wickedness" were not the worst in absolutism. Far more sinister was its essence: "a studied philosophy of crime."

Resistance to Absolutism and the Rise of English Liberty

In the long-term process of strengthening royal power and the assertiveness of the modern state, civic activity by privileged estates, provinces, towns, and professional corporations was undermined and annihilated step by step. As a result, absolute monarchy seemed utterly unshakable and secure in its might. And yet it eventually crumbled into dust, although torrents of blood were a customary price for its fall. Historiography usually indicates the development of liberal ideas as a main cause of that fall. Acton does not deny this but makes an original claim that the Protestant sects played a crucial role in the active resistance against the modern state and in the battle of ideas that led to liberalism's rise. It was through "the combined efforts of the weak . . . to resist the reign of force and constant wrong, that, in the rapid change but slow progress of four hundred years, liberty [was] preserved, and secured, and extended, and finally understood."

In early modern Europe, the persecution of religious dissenters and the protection of their own church were ordinary policies for Catholic and Protestant states. However, both kinds of states persecuted Protestants who did not belong to one of the new "mainline" churches: the Anglicans, Lutherans, and Calvinists.

The Anabaptists, Socinians, Armenians, Huguenots, Puritans, Presbyterians, Congregationalists, Quakers, and other sects had no chance of establishing their own state-supported churches. Therefore, they were increasingly turning against a state church (a veritable Babylon in their view) as well as an arbitrary state as such. However terrible, their religious fanaticism was necessary to generate energy and determination capable of resisting the equally strong drive of the modern state toward unlimited power.

According to Acton, the sectarians, along with Calvinists of various shades (when they did not hold power), belonged to the chief forces standing behind the revolts and wars of the sixteenth and seventeenth centuries, which were ostensibly of a religious nature but actually had more of a political character. This struggle began in France (1559–1598), intensified after the massacre of St. Bartholomew's Day (1572) and in the Netherlands (1566–1587), and ended in England (1642–1660, 1688). The sectarians as well as the Catholic opponents of Protestant monarchy in France revived the medieval right of armed resistance against unjust government and of deposing tyrants; restored an even older belief in the right of a nation to control power; demanded freedom of worship; and dreamed about the kind of self-rule that prevailed among the ancient Israelites after they had settled in the Promised Land. "The greater part of the political ideas of Milton, Locke, and Rousseau, may be found in the ponderous Latin of Jesuits. . . . The ideas were there, and were taken up when it suited them by extreme adherents of Rome and of Geneva," that is, by the Catholics and the Calvinists. Yet, as Acton adds, these ideas "produced no lasting fruit, until a century after the Reformation." If so, this raises the question of why. What prevented them from achieving a lasting effect?

The answer to these questions leads us to Acton's other assertion that the ideas that the sectarians animated or created remained dormant until they passed through a secularization that separated them from their religious roots and the fanatism of their framers. It was only "when they renounced their theological parentage, and were translated into the scientific term of politics, [that] they conquered and spread over the nations as general truths." The crucial step in this transformation from religious to political conflict—from the Reformation to the revolutions—took place in England after the restoration of the Stuarts to the English throne in 1660. The next stage in this process was the Glorious Revolution (1688), but its ideas, although secularized, still retained their national character as the rights of Englishmen. The subsequent stages—the American Revolution (1775) and the French Revolution (1789)—adopted them as "general truths" of universal application to all humankind, not as "British exports." Let us look briefly at the first two stages.

The Puritans and other Nonconformists (i.e., the dissenters from the Anglican Church—Baptists, Congregationalists, Presbyterians, Quakers, and others) were the chief driving force behind the changes that took place in mid-seventeenth-century England. It was not them, however, but the gentry and the Anglican clergy who were the main beneficiaries of these changes. Test Acts—designed to eliminate the Catholics from public life—discriminated against all who did not follow the established church, including the Nonconformists. In turn, electoral law privileged landowners, which gave the gentry control over the House of Commons. The period between 1660 and 1688 was "the era in which parties took the place of churches as a political force."

From its beginning, the emerging political scene in England was bipolar. On one side were the future Tories, originally known as the Court Party; on the other was the Country Party, the future Whigs. The first grouped conservative gentry, clergy, and lawyers who out of fear of disorder and a new revolution supported the monarchy and "that which Hobbes called Leviathan, meaning the abstract notion of the State." To be eligible for office, they pledged to not resist royal authority and to consider passive obedience as the only permissible means of opposition. The members of the second group did not differ socially from the first and did not like armed resistance either. They also preferred the policy of expediency and sought a compromise. They did not, however, exclude active disobedience if the king violated fundamental laws. They appreciated the value of traditional rights as preserved on old parchments and justified the rebellion of their ancestors against Charles I, the beheaded king (1649).

The Stuarts who returned to the English throne, Charles II and his brother James II, proved to be incorrigible, on top of being awkward. As a result, the dynasty, reinvited in 1660, was expelled from England in 1688 and Parliament invited in new rulers, William of Orange and his wife Mary, the daughter of the last king. On account of its bloodless course and achievements, this brief rebellion is known in British history as the Glorious Revolution. The new order established as a result of this revolution dispelled any doubt as to who was the sovereign and who could reign, provided that the ruler obeyed the law of the land. "Parliament became supreme in administration as well as in legislation. The king became its servant on good behaviour, liable to dismissal for himself or his ministers. . . . Authority was limited and regulated and controlled."

Acton notes that the change that the Glorious Revolution introduced was slight, mainly addressing past wrongs and leaving power in the same hands—the monarchy and aristocratic families. It therefore did not preclude the possibility of a return to continental ways of governing. However slight, the change proved sufficiently strong to steer England's regime onto the path of slow adjustment that eliminated its weaknesses, developed a full separation of powers, and ensured civil liberties. Ultimately, English constitutionalism originated what Acton calls "mature liberty," that is, the liberal order of an evolutionary kind. As mentioned, he also termed it a "liberty founded on inequality," but, with the gradual extension of voting rights implemented in the nineteenth century, it certainly approached the American pattern of "liberty founded on equality."

On the occasion of reviewing the evolution of Whiggism after the Glorious Revolution, Acton emphasizes that it has always had two currents: one coming from constitutional lawyers such as John Selden (1584–1654), Baron John Somers (1651–1716), and from Burke; and another linked to the Roundheads (opponents of Charles I), John Milton (1608–1674), Locke, and Macaulay. The first strand stressed natural law and the laws of the country that bind both the government and the people, including its representatives in Parliament, and treated armed resistance as the last resort in the event of the king violating fundamental law. The second group was not only more radical but also prone to "the generalisations of an ordinary Liberalism." It placed the people in the same role in which the divine right theory placed the monarchy, giving them absolute sovereignty—that is, not far from the Athenian-like tyranny of numbers. There is no question which of these currents is closer to Acton's heart. And it is mainly this current that during the conflict with American colonists endowed Whiggism with a more universal character—the rights of man—overcoming a narrow concept of the rights of Englishmen.

As for the Tories, Acton acknowledges that they "underwent many developments" after the Glorious Revolution but does not elaborate on the nature of these developments. It is as if he had not grasped the meaning of Burke's switch from the Whigs to the Tories, taking with him a large part of the Whiggish tradition that Acton appreciated the most. In some of his letters, Acton confesses that liberalism is for him like a religion and that he is "a narrow doctrinaire" in this respect. Was this what prevented him from commenting on the merger of the Whigs with the philosophical radicals in the mid-1800s when the Liberal Party was founded, thus shifting significantly toward the very brand of liberalism he loathed?

Two Different Revolutions, American and French

As mentioned, Acton viewed the entire early modern period as a fierce fight against the growing usurpation of the modern state and a slow movement toward mature liberty. This four-hundred-year-long process from the Reformation to the revolutions culminated in the American and French Revolutions. We will now briefly examine this culmination to see if these revolutions were similar or not, and if they contributed equally to the advancement of liberty.

America

As mentioned in chapter 2, Acton emphasizes that the American colonists (at first mostly Puritans) enjoyed the freedom to arrange their public life from the beginning of their settlements in the New World. They owed it to a combination of several factors. First, the Stuarts granted them liberal charters because their government wanted to get rid of religious and political dissenters. Second, the Puritan colonists quickly extended their custom of having the faithful run parishes to the handling of the affairs of their settlements. As a result, the sectarians turned into citizens and gained the chance to put their political ideas in practice. Third, they built up their self-government, starting from their towns and ending in the colonial assembly. Fourth, colonial laws and taxes were of their own making because, until the eve of the revolution, the colonies were left alone without much interference from London. For Acton, these features of colonial order in America represented pure liberalism of an evolutionary kind.

The quiet development of American colonies ended when the British attempted to reaffirm their control over them after their victories in the Seven Years' War (1756–1763). Imposing new taxes on the colonies was an efficient way to do so, because it was unquestionably legal: the letter of the law was on the side of Parliament. In defense of their freedom, the colonists initially invoked the rights of Englishmen, in particular the principle of no taxation without representation. Later, when they realized that Parliament was refusing to acknowledge their rights, they appealed to a higher, natural law: "By the laws of God and nature, government must not raise taxes on the property of the people without the consent of the people or their deputies. There can be no prescription old enough to supersede the law of Nature and the grant of God Almighty, who has given all men a right to be free." And finally, when that did not help and, worse, the British started using brutal force, they resorted to revolution. Their struggle did not only have a military dimension but also extended to the world of ideas. The Declaration of Independence (1776) no longer referred to the rights of Englishmen; it boldly proclaimed "the rights of man" and gave them a more secular foundation.

Keeping the above in mind, the first phase of the American Revolution—the War of Independence (1775–1783)—was a natural step in the growth of civic liberty. It aimed not at the destruction of what had been built before but at the removal of barriers to its organic growth. The second phase (1783–1789), in turn, was a milestone in the development of mature liberty. It undertook the formidable task of building a new nation based on rights, designed the Constitution that combined liberty and equality, and formed the most stable political regime in human history.

In his review of this process, Acton mostly ignores the War of Independence and focuses on the second phase of the revolution, in particular the Constitutional Convention (1787). He stresses that at this stage the revolution ceased to appeal to radical, universal, and democratic ideas and took a cautious and compromising approach. Moreover, it acquired an antidemocratic character, which was especially visible at the convention. The delegates did their utmost to limit the direct impact of the voters' will on the government, restrain majority rule, and protect minorities, understood either as individuals or as states in a new union. To do so and to find a compromise between a variety of interests, particularly between large and small states, the convention designed constitutions that balanced government in all possible ways. It applied not only the modern division of powers in accordance with Montesquieu's prescription (legislative, executive, and judicial branches) but also the ancient division according to the ruling principle (the rule of one, a few, and the many, i.e., the president, the Senate, and the House of Representatives), as well as the division between national and state governments (federalism), indirect presidential election (Acton deemed this an insufficient, halfway solution), and the Supreme Court ruling on the constitutionality of law. Furthermore, the Bill of Rights (ratified by 1791) supplemented the US Constitution by safeguarding civil rights and confirming states' rights. In this way the process of building the legal foundation of the United States of America was completed.

Acton loved all the divisions and checks on the government and voiced his utmost admiration for American fundamental law. Noticing its weaknesses—mainly the retention of slavery and insufficiently defined states' rights—he particularly commended federalism as the best check on absolute democracy: "[America] had solved with astonishing and unexampled success two problems which had hitherto baffled the capacity of the most enlightened nations: they had contrived a system of federal government which prodigiously increased the national power and yet respected local liberties and authorities; and they had founded it on the principle of equality, without surrendering the securities for property and freedom. I call their success unexampled, not because it is a forcible term, but because it exactly indicates the peculiar character of the history of the American Constitution, and its special significance for ourselves."

France

If America was for Acton an exemplary case for civic liberty, France was its opposite, representing "the classic land of absolutism," whose penchant for arbitrary rule could be traceable even to ancient Rome. Early modern France was run top-down from at least the seventeenth century, with civic activity nearly extinguished, but continued maintaining a fiction of the medieval society of estates (the clergy, the nobility, and the commoners), in which each estate had separate functions and therefore different rights and duties. The two higher estates kept their social and economic privileges but lost their political role and, in Tocqueville's words, were changed into an idle caste. Worse, from a bastion against centralization and arbitrary power, they turned into supporters of the throne and a mainstay of absolutism.

Although modern, the French state did retain some medieval features: it was not a uniform state with the same law throughout the country but an aggregation of provinces, each with separate statutes, institutions, and taxes. Moreover, provincial *parlements* (courts) preserved remnants of the independence and civic spirit they inherited from the Middle Ages. France's provincial separatism somewhat resembled colonial America: until the American Revolution, the thirteen colonies constituted separate political entities, notwithstanding their similarities.

Absolute in theory, the French monarchy was becoming progressively weaker in the second half of the eighteenth century. Financial crisis was the most visible sign of its increasing impotence—the king could not make provinces share their tax burden more equally and the privileged estates increase their taxes and thereby reduce the budget deficit and debt. The vanishing prestige of the monarchy was, however, much more menacing for the ancien régime. Acton emphasizes the role of French *philosophes* in deriding and undermining the existing order. The contractarian theory of civil society and state and the inalienable rights common to all that the *philosophes* promoted made the still semifeudal social arrangements and the state thoroughly illegitimate. The Glorious Revolution and, above all, the more recent American Revolution and its political ideas set a tempting example for the French.

The desperate Louis XVI appealed in 1787 to the Assembly of Notables (a council of aristocrats and high clerics) for help in resolving dire financial problems. The notables, however, rejected higher taxes on themselves and instead advised the king to call the Estates General—that is, the representation of France's three estates—which had not been convened since 1614. The king acquiesced: he summoned the estates that were elected on the basis of nearly universal although unequal male suffrage; moreover, he encouraged a prelim-

The September Massacres of political prisoners in Paris and the newly elected National Convention (September 1792) opened the next chapter of revolutionary violence. The convention formally ended monarchy, established a republic, sent the king to the guillotine (January 1793), and instituted the Reign of Terror, of which the Gironde became one of the first victims. The liberal phase of the Revolution was over: the Revolution turned into the despotism of the Jacobins, led initially by Georges Danton (1759–1794) and Maximilien Robespierre (1758–1794), and then, after the former was guillotined, solely by the latter. It was also a dictatorship of Paris over the more conservative provinces, exercised by commissars (Acton calls them "proconsuls") sent out across France with the power of life and death. It was these proconsuls who, fearing for their safety, overthrew the despot and sent him to the guillotine (July 1794).

The so-called Thermidorian Reaction that followed the demise of Robespierre did not mean a return to the order set by one of previous revolutionary constitutions or to the ancien régime. It did, however, mean the end of the Terror and a slow process of taking away "power from the unworthy hands of the men who destroyed Robespierre." Some of the main culprits were guillotined. The convention could not prevent it after a large group of deputies (mostly Girondins) took their seats back in December.

One of the most important tasks of the convention was to draft a new constitution. The Constitution of 1791 was not fitting, because France was no longer a monarchy; the Jacobin Constitution of 1793 was never implemented, and no one wanted to revive it in 1794. The convention thus prepared another constitution (August 1795) that better suited the existing reality. Having learned the price of unlimited revolutionary power, the deputies now stressed restricting and dividing the government. They created a two-chamber legislature, a directory of five as the executive, and two-stage elections with property requirements. The last act of the deputies was to secure their own position in the next legislature, two-thirds of which was to be selected out of the members of the convention. The revolt of monarchists against this blatant dictate was crushed by Napoleon Bonaparte, a young general with a Jacobin past and a great future.

Here Acton ends his lectures on the French Revolution, as if he believed that the Revolution was over. Whether he was right or not is of secondary importance: it is his assessment of the Revolution that matters. As mentioned, he admired the work of the National Assembly and the Constitution of September 1791, various reservations notwithstanding. The remaining years of the Revolution did not arouse his enthusiasm. At this point he preferred to hide his attitude, although his coded language occasionally betrayed his disgust for what was transpiring in France. In the main, he detested the Revolution's betrayal of liberty for the sake of equality and the abuse of power and terror as a by-product. Curiously, he did not attempt to assess the Revolution in general. With the exception of the Reign of Terror, he probably still considered it better than the ancien régime. What is certain, however, is his lack of enthusiasm for the French Revolution, as displayed in his assessment of the American Revolution.

The Aftermath of the Revolutions

The process from the Reformation to the revolutions ended in the nineteenth century as the aftermath of the age of revolution. What was its impact on liberty and liberalism? Did it advance liberalism of the organic-evolutionary kind or its constructivist-doctrinaire version? Let us take a quick look at this development both in Europe and in America.

Europe

The French Revolution, even in its liberal period, did not see the tension between equality and liberty; on the contrary, "liberty, which had been known only in the form of privilege, was . . . identified with equality." In its efforts to advance both goals, the Revolution chose the method of rapid change: the new regime quickly did away with estate privileges, serfdom, provincial rights, and absolute monarchy. This greatly increased equality and raised the legal and social position of most of the French, therefore affecting their personal freedom as well. The French Constitution of 1791 was the product of such attitudes and policies and set the pattern for continental, constructivist liberalism in the nineteenth century.

Acton approved the work of the National Assembly that designed the constitution, but also noticed its poisonous fruit. For the price for swift change was an all-powerful central government without checks and balances. Consequently, the Revolution substituted absolute monarchy with another, more absolute power: that of the people. As sovereign, the people had the right to change whatever they wished, regardless of time-sanctioned laws and institutions and the rights of intermediary bodies, such as the church and provinces. ("The substance of the ideas of 1789 is not the limitation of the sovereign power, but the abrogation of intermediate powers.") Worse still, it gave unlimited power to the people abstractly understood. The real power rested in the hands of an omnipotent legislature that represented the state. As individuals, the people were powerless, exercising their sovereignty at the ballot box every few years. Acton formed his objection to such arrangements in these words: "All authority comes from the people, to be concentrated in the State. No secondary authorities limit, no laws regulate, the action of the supreme will. The powers that rule the State . . . reject all authority which does not proceed from the uniform principle on which they rest; and there is no security and no stability in their laws, however favourable their disposition may be. An absolute parliament is less to be relied on than an absolute monarch; because where it has the will to do wrong, it has always the power."

As mentioned in chapter 2, Acton saw society as a living organism, composed of myriad interest groups, localities, corporations, and institutions, each having its own legitimate sphere of work, and each competing with others, but all operating within the law guarded by the state. The state is to act as an impartial arbiter that enforces fair game but does not compress society "like a thumbscrew." The ideas and policies that transpired from the French Revolution and its Constitution of 1791 promoted the exact opposite. The state (government) acts according to abstract principles and imposes them on society; it thus becomes like "a mould, into which society is forced to pour itself." European liberalism adopted that attitude as its own and attempted to put it into practice.

As examples of such policies in action, Acton lists France between 1815 and 1848 and Italy after 1848. Both enforced top-down order, ignoring or breaking the will of the people. By excluding the overwhelming majority of the people from the right to vote, France made a mockery of the principle of representation, while in Italy, its process of "unification" was in fact a brutal conquest of the south by the north and the coercion of various peoples—who had lived separately for about 1,500 years—to live together under a law that was not of their own making. In other words, Italy had to pass through a process that had taken place in France during the Revolution.

The second offshoot of the French Revolution was nationalism. Originally, liberalism and nationalism were indistinguishable from each other, both emphasizing popular sovereignty. Nationalism, however, aimed at national rights, understood as independence (self-determination) and ethnic solidarity, while liberalism sought individual rights. Leaving aside its Polish origins, nationalism was animated by Napoleon and the armies of the French Revolution, who carried the lofty slogans of equality and liberty throughout Europe but also brought the violence and plunder typical of war. This awakened a national consciousness among ordinary people seeking either unification in one state (Italy, Germany) or independence from foreign domination. These hopes were suppressed by the Congress of Vienna in 1815–1816, which entirely ignored national principle and relied on dynastic and state interest.

In the second phase of its development after the Congress of Vienna, nationalism still protested more against misgovernment than national oppression. This changed in the third stage of its maturation, occurring around the time of the Spring of Nations (1848–1849), when nationalism became a powerful, revolutionary force. It then made the national principle supreme, endowing the nation the same elevated position that the French Revolution gave to the people. Furthermore, it claimed that the nation has the right to all its territory and cannot "allow a part of itself to belong to a foreign State, or the whole to be divided into several native States." Consequently, nationalism turned into a subversive idea, as it questioned nearly all existing borders throughout Europe.

As mentioned in chapter 2, Acton calls nationalism embodying these ideas "national unity" and contrasts it with national liberty.

While the latter represents the most advanced version of Acton's best practical regime, providing rights and securities to all its inhabitants regardless of nationality, the former is a menace to order and civilization. He sums up this line of judgment in strong terms: "The theory of nationality is more absurd and more criminal than the theory of socialism."

America

In the period from the inception of the Union to the years immediately following the Civil War—Acton did not write on postbellum America—the United States experienced a steady expansion of national government and federal bureaucracy, as well as growing differences and conflicts between the predominantly urban and industrial states in the North and the chiefly rural and agricultural states in the South. Simultaneously, America suffered from a slow erosion of its strong civic communities and their self-reliance, so characteristic of colonial times. In other words, it increasingly abandoned its civic liberty (and evolutionary, organic liberalism) and accepted doctrinaire liberalism, with its penchant for the pursuit of abstract principles and governmental fiat. Although this process was much less rapid and advanced than in continental Europe, the United States was not free from it.

Acton traces the beginning of this process to the third American president, Thomas Jefferson (1743–1826), who was in office from 1801 to 1809. Unlike his predecessors, who had viewed the presidency as standing above political disputes, Jefferson saw it as his duty to enforce the democratic will, even if he personally disagreed with it. He was also the first to test the power of national government by the Embargo Act, which Congress enacted in 1807. Whether this policy was justified or not is a secondary matter (the act was soon repealed). What is important is that the federal government could impose its will despite a firm opposition, in this case from the Northern states. Once the test of strength proved effective, the government began to treat its use as an ordinary policy.

In 1816 the national government passed tariffs to protect domestic industries. They were strongly supported by the North but opposed by the South, whose cotton was mainly sold abroad and could be hurt by retaliatory duties. The tariffs were drastically increased in 1828 (and reduced in 1833) and raised again in 1842, thereby deepening the division within the Union. Another consequence of this policy was an increase in the tax revenue that was spent on "internal improvements," that is, roads, canals, and other investments in various localities. This strengthened the position of the national administration vis-à-vis the states, which the South did not like, seeing it as another intrusion into its life. Acton also mentions the "spoils system" as yet another method of governmental expansion. The system allowed political supporters to be rewarded with public posts, originally on a small scale. George Washington dismissed nine officials in eight years and Jefferson did it thirty-nine times, while around the time of the Civil War such patronage reached about sixty thousand people.

The growing conflict between national government and the Southern states also had a constitutional dimension, in which the question of slavery began to play an increasingly central role. As for the constitutional issue, it concerned the question of whether states had the right to nullify federal law and ultimately reclaim their sovereignty. Acton sided with the advocates of state rights because, like his mentor Tocqueville, he always looked with suspicion at central government and upheld self-rule. For him, this was a dispute between civic liberty and federal administration. As for slavery, he denounced the US Constitution for not abolishing it, but before and during the Civil War, he viewed it again as a clash of civic liberty, this time against an abstract tenet. The "rabid" abolitionists reduced the entire conflict to one issue—slavery—and demanded that the government act on principle, whatever the costs. According to Acton, slavery should have been regulated step by step so that at certain point it would not differ from hired labor, instead of the head-on crush that ended in a bloody war.

Acton observes that the policy of benefiting one segment of the people at the cost of others leads to social conflicts that, if not resolved, end up in revolution and violent regime change, while distributing advantages and disadvantages to geographically different regions can lead to civil war and ultimately to secession. This is how he saw the conflict between the North and the South. In the 1850s, both sides no longer sought compromise but rather turned into two hostile nations, differing in many respects, in which context slavery was only one of many sources of division. The victorious presidential election of Abraham Lincoln (1860), a stanch enemy of state separatism and slavery, was the signal for the secession of the South and then the Civil War (1861–1865).

The Confederate States of America adopted a constitution—provisional in March 1861, final in February 1862—that mirrored the US Constitution except for the issues that had been the subject of long-term contention between the South and the North. Thus, it clearly declared the following: the Confederation is made up of sovereign states; the federal government must not impose taxes and duties that favor some regions and industries at the expense of others; and the patronage system is illegal, as are internal improvements, except for safety reasons and regulation of waterways. Acton praised it as an exemplary case of liberalism and civic liberty, seeing slavery as the only serious flaw in it:

> The political ideas of the Confederacy . . . justify me, I think, in saying that history can show no instance of so great an effort made by Republicans to remedy the faults of that form of government. Had they adopted the means which would have ensured and justified success, had they called on the negroes to be partners with them in the perils of war and in the fruits of victory, I believe that generous resolution would have conferred in all future ages incalculable blessings on the human race. They would have supplied the advocates of freedom hereafter with a peerless model. They would have realised the ideals of its friends and disarmed the resistance of its foes.

He contrasted the South's attempt to establish a truly liberal regime with the introduction of martial law in the North and mobilization of all resources for war. He interpreted it as a rapid descent to "pure democracy and the absolute supremacy of the people" as well as a triumph of abstract principles and a doctrinaire brand of liberalism. His remarks about the United States written in 1861 and 1866 were very harsh:

> We may consult the history of the American Union to understand the true history of republicanism, and the danger of mistaking it. It is simply the spurious democracy of the French Revolution that has destroyed the Union, by disintegrating the remnants of English traditions and institutions. . . . The secession of the Southern States . . . is chiefly important . . . as a protest and reaction against revolutionary doctrines, and as a move in the opposite direction to that which prevails in Europe.

> The spurious liberty of the United States is twice cursed, for it deceives those whom it attracts and those whom it repels. By exhibiting the spectacle of a people claiming to be free, but whose love of freedom means hatred of inequality, jealousy of limitations to power, and reliance on the State as an instrument to mould as well

> as to control society, it calls on its admirers to hate aristocracy and teaches its adversaries to fear the people. The North has used the doctrines of Democracy to destroy self-government. The South applied the principle of conditional federation to cure the evils and correct the errors of a false interpretation of Democracy.

Yet, despite his condemnation of American democracy and the winning side, Acton also found some redeeming qualities in America. He saw them in restraining from postwar vengeance and in treating the vanquished, in particular the commander of the Confederate army, General Robert E. Lee, graciously. Commending President Andrew Johnson for this policy, he concluded that "it is too soon to despair of a community that has among its leading citizens such men as these."

His evaluation of the American regime in general somewhat softened about thirty years later when he delivered lectures on modern history. The concluding chapter of the printed collection is on the American Revolution. Reviewing the US Constitution, he points out its great points as well as its weak ones. Among the latter he condemns "the absence of a definition of State Rights [that] led to the most sanguinary civil war of modern times." Still, the last sentence is this chapter runs as follows: "And yet, by the development of the principle of Federalism, it has produced a community more powerful, more prosperous, more intelligent, and more free than any other which the world has seen."

WHAT STRIKES THE READER the most in Acton's history of freedom is his emphasis on the value of tradition in the development of liberty. He dismisses the idea popular among early modern liberals that civil liberties (inalienable rights) are based on an inherent, genuine freedom that supposedly existed in the state of nature. According to him, liberty is not a raw freedom that individuals could have enjoyed at the beginning of history (if such an anarchic freedom ever occurred); on the contrary, it is "a delicate fruit of a mature civilization," that is, the product of long development that may eventually lead to mature, ordered liberty. His other metaphors underline this quality of freedom as well: it grows like a plant or develops like a language. Furthermore, it cannot come all at once, through a revolution, as many tend to believe, but only through a slow evolution. As he stresses on the occasion of reviewing Israelite liberty, national tradition that organically grows is one of two fundamental principles on which all freedom rests (a higher law being the second). Revolution, in turn, is a frenzy that threatens a nation's existence. It is akin to national suicide.

Despite this unequivocal condemnation of revolution, he seems to recognize the necessity of violent change that occurs from time to time in history. This can be seen in his remarks on the fall of Rome, on the violent shocks that accompanied the passage from the Middle Ages to the early modern period, and especially on the French Revolution. Rome's despotism and French absolutism were dead ends as far as freedom is concerned and had to be overthrown. The Middle Ages also needed violent shocks; otherwise they would have continued their life in "a twilight of fiction" and rough inequality. If so, did we catch Acton in a lack of consistency?

This question can be properly addressed if we look at his evaluation of the effects of these upheavals. The fall of Rome ended a terrible despotism but at the cost of a rapid collapse of civilization, followed by a painfully long recovery in the early Middle Ages. The early modern period got rid of medieval myths and vassalage and brought about a great revival of art and science but was attended by the rise of arbitrary rule and religious wars, ultimately ending in absolutism. In turn, the French Revolution abolished absolute monarchy but also led to terror, corrupt power, and Napoleonic turmoil, followed by the triumph of doctrinaire liberalism, gradually eclipsing evolutionary liberalism. Were the results worth the cost of these violent changes? Acton is not clear about this. What is clear, however, is that he is not being inconsistent when he strongly condemns revolutions, especially when it entails not a quick and brief shake-up of the status quo but a regime of continual change.

Another striking point in Acton's history of liberty is his periodization. He mentions twice the four-hundred-year periods crucial for freedom, the first in the Middle Ages and the second in the early modern period, ending in his own time. He does not specify exactly when they begin and when they end; moreover, these four-hundred-year periods must be taken as approximations. If so, and if we proceed backward from around 1900, we have the span from the nineteenth century back to the fifteenth, coinciding with the beginning of early modernity. The next phase took place between the fifteenth century and the eleventh. Were we to continue this temporal regression, we would have another four- or five-century period between the beginning of the High Middle Ages and the collapse of Rome. Consequently, liberty in Western civilization passes through a series of sequences lasting roughly four centuries. The first is marked by the collapse of civilization and chaos but also by the disappearance of Roman despotism; the second is distinguished by the development of medieval freedom, with its fragmentation of power, urban and provincial self-government, but also drastic inequality; and the third is overshadowed by religious wars and absolutism but also by a parallel outburst of resistance of the "weak," the birth of liberalism, and mature liberty.

This brings us to yet another of Acton's original assertions that the tremendous rise of arbitrary power in early modern times would have been irresistible were it not for the fanaticism of the weak, that is, religious dissenters from the mainline Protestant churches (but not excluding Catholics fighting against the prospect of Huguenot monarchy in France). They were ready to resist the state-imposed church ("Babylon") no matter what it took. Moreover, he argues that the birth of liberalism owed a great deal to the struggle of the sectarians and their appeal to old civic ideas, be they Hebrew or medieval, which rapidly spread among the educated elite and politically active classes as soon as these ideas had shed their religious tinge.

As for liberalism itself, Acton's history of liberty shows two conflicting liberalisms, one grounded in national tradition and a higher law and another appealing to abstract principles and not averse to employing coercion to adjust reality to its ideas. Acton firmly favors the former and repudiates the latter, claiming that it is not liberalism but an impostor.

As mentioned, evolutionary liberalism emerges spontaneously in local communities as civic liberty and evolves on the basis of national tradition—provided it has seeds of liberty at its beginning, basically popular sovereignty—and the recognition of a higher law. Such an organic, genuine liberalism can appear even in premodern times (Providence ceaselessly supports liberty) but achieves the early stages of mature liberty only with the Whigs around the time of the Glorious Revolution. In time, it evolves from liberty in inequality to liberty in equality and continues its evolution because it does not have preordained ends, except for maintaining civic freedom. National tradition that does not acknowledge popular sovereignty, or does so in defective ways, cannot evolve into a liberty-friendly regime. Ancient Rome is a good example. Unlike the Greek *polis*, the Roman Republic had a flawed popular sovereignty, being a de facto oligarchy. The empire got rid of it altogether and evolved into a despotism that continued in existence until the fall of Constantinople in 1453.

As for doctrinaire liberalism, it developed and flourished on the European continent then dominated by absolute monarchy. Deprived of experience in practical politics, early modern political thinkers favored general theories and abstract principles, such as state of nature, original liberty and equality, and the social contract. The French Revolution transformed this liberalism into a political practice and infected continental Europe with it. Eventually, it was not only continental Europe or Europe as such that embraced this kind of liberalism; America did so too during and after the Civil War. We may add that this process continued in the twentieth century—that is, after Acton's death—accelerating in particular as a result of World War I and II. Human reason is predisposed to accept general formulas and principles that appear rational and finds it difficult to resist them in the long run.

Although Acton studied liberty in the past, the lesson he learned from history holds true for our time as well. It is up to us if we want to take advantage of it or not. We ought to answer ourselves if we are aware of the inherent flaws of democracy and willing to look for ways to curb it. Do we rely on our own efforts and the activity of our local communities to resolve our problems, or are we seeking assistance from the national government as the first, rather than the last, resort? Do we respect time-honored laws, institutions, and customs and firmly believe that our problems can be solved in small steps and in conformity with our tradition or do we prefer a rapid change, regardless of risks, that will deal with the challenges of our life once and for all? These questions are not abstract, but, depending on our answers, they affect our views on Acton's teachings.

4

Reception and Legacy

One cannot be surprised when a person of strong convictions, even one as reserved as Acton, proves to be controversial and evaluation of his complex legacy varies widely, from admiration to derision. To bring some order to contradictory opinions about Acton's thought, we will consider separately views that prevailed immediately after his death and those that evaluated his impact from a greater temporal distance. We will further split the longer-term perspectives into two categories: first, those concerning his legacy as a historian, and second, those reviewing his legacy as a political thinker, especially with regard to liberty and its history. Finally, we will summarize the negative assessment of Acton's ideas and take a look at the most recent publications by and about Acton, both his own writings and works that evaluate his thought.

After his death, the public showed intense curiosity about the "enigmatic" figure of Baron Acton who had aroused so much enthusiasm among University of Cambridge dons and students. He was still little known outside the circle of his international friends and English intellectual and political elites; furthermore, he was perceived as a "bookworm, a walking Dictionary" who "devoured books and accumulated facts" but did not publish anything of importance. At least, this is the picture of him that emerged from published obituaries. The editors of Acton's works in this early period had a twofold task: first, to bring his ideas to the general public, and second, to revise this image.

Acton's Reception until the Late 1920s

During the fifteen years following his death, there was an avalanche of publications of his works, both previously published and unpublished, which presented a significant portion of Acton's writing, including some letters. These were the Cambridge lectures on modern history and the French Revolution, his letters to various people, particularly to Mary Drew (Prime Minister Gladstone's daughter), and collections of his more important articles. The sheer number of these publications (seven books in fifteen years) undermines the view that Acton wrote next to nothing. Furthermore, these books included lengthy introductions by their editors that portrayed his life and attempted to evaluate his legacy. These introductions, as well as other early reviews of his life and work, generated a very positive, even flattering, image of Lord Acton.

The publications written between the time of his death and the late 1920s stressed, first of all, the breadth and depth of his knowledge, not only in history but also in theology, biblical criticism, philosophy, and political and economic thought (though not in poetry, literature, or exact sciences). His mastery of the fields that comprise the humanities allowed him to discuss them on equal terms with scholars who specialized in any one of those fields. If his knowledge of ancient and medieval history was "less minute," it became "wonderfully full and exact when it reached the Renaissance and Reformation periods." In fact, as one of his friends enthusiastically claimed, "no Englishman has ever surpassed Lord Acton in his knowledge of Modern History."

The next issue that these early publications addressed was Acton's image as a "dry-as-dust" figure who "passed no judgment, framed no generalizations." The reviewers claimed just the opposite: he was passionate and inspiring, and always standing on the side of "principles over interests, of liberty over tyranny, of truth over all forms of evasion and equivocation." Furthermore, he did not shy away from passing judgments, even severe judgments, which can be linked to his adherence to a strict moral code. "His scholarship was to him as practical as his politics, and his politics as ethical as his faith." Thus, the question was not that Acton "passed no judgment, framed no generalizations" but that his strong moral code made him precisely judgmental and prone to sweeping, sometimes far-fetched, generalizations.

As mentioned, Acton had in mind an outline of the history of liberty even if in the end he could not pour it out on paper. Regretting this loss, some reviewers noticed that his insights relating to freedom are visible in other writings. He defined liberty mainly as the right to do what one ought to do. Consequently, morality and the freedom to act according to its dictates became crucial in his view of politics and history, as they provided criteria for the evaluation of the past and the present. As a result, he disdained Machiavellian politics and strongly condemned all those who had practiced it. Politics cannot be divorced from morality.

The reviewers also stressed that Acton warned against undivided power. It was as dangerous in the Roman Empire as it is in modern democracy, where it can lead to the tyranny of the majority. His ideal of liberty seemed essentially English (Whiggish), even if it was "less partisan . . . [and] insular." In the spirit of 1688, he understood it as respect for law, custom, and tradition. "He had none of the blindly doctrinaire idealism of the continental liberal." What surprised some, however, was his claim that the conflict between the empire and the papacy in the Middle Ages and medieval political thought rendered great services to freedom. For were this view right, Catholicism would have had more intimate links to the cause of liberty than did the Reformation, which restricted freedom instead of enlarging it and brought conflicts, wars, and strong monarchies. For English—or, more generally, Protestant—readers this was an odd, if not outrageous, statement, and yet, in light of Acton's strong criticism of the Catholic Church and the papacy, his views could not be easily dismissed as Catholic bias. And this was just one of many controversial views held by "his lordship."

Acton's Legacy as a Historian

As mentioned in chapter 1, Acton's tenure at the University of Cambridge brought significant changes to the scholarship and teaching of history, not only at that university but also in England more widely. As an ardent student of Leopold von Ranke (1795–1886), he aimed at objective history, detached "from the temporary and [the] transient," and searching for the truth about the past as a goal in itself, not as an auxiliary tool for politics, philosophy, law, and other pursuits. Like Ranke, he emphasized the need for the study of archival sources and stressed (probably more than did his master) the importance of ideas over great individuals in the fundamental movements in history.

In promoting Ranke's methodology, Acton differed from him in important ways. Not only was Acton not dry and colorless or sparing in making judgments, but he also treated history as a sort of supreme moral tribunal that put past heroes on trial for their crimes. He believed that historians are not bound by the common law principle "that innocence must be assumed until guilt is proven.

The presumption which is favourable to makers of history is adverse to writers of history." Yet, historians often do just the opposite and, as mentioned before, they resort to "hero worship," which he found intolerable. Because "history deals considerably with hanging matter," deep distrust of witnesses and official (state) accounts were axiomatic for him. In other words, he demanded critical and thorough evaluation of primary sources.

Acton's approach to research and the teaching of history was treated at Cambridge as "the breviary of historians" and permeated at that institution for a generation after his death. History ceased to be just a series of biographies of great figures, a discipline auxiliary to other fields, but began to be researched and studied for its own sake, with all the methodological tools that Ranke and Acton advocated. Its position did certainly improve at the University of Cambridge, where it was no longer considered as "a second-class subject" inappropriate for the brightest students.

Acton was aware that his positions on the importance of universal ethical standards, the role of history as a moral tribunal, and the historian as a "hanging judge" were controversial. As he stated in the inaugural lecture in 1895, "The weight of opinion is against me when I exhort you never to debase the moral currency." Still earlier, this is how he had excused his silence in the 1880s and why his history of liberty became the "Madonna of the Future." Even in the late nineteenth century, the predominant attitude among historians—gradually evolving into consensus—was that they ought not to be judgmental and apply their ethical standards onto the past. Acton thus exposed himself to an easy criticism that was growing as the memory of his charismatic personality was waning. By the late 1920s and early 1930s, the idea of moral judgments in history seemed entirely abandoned by historians at Cambridge as well as elsewhere.

The leading and devastating attack on Acton as a historian and his methodology came from University of Cambridge professor Herbert Butterfield. As a student in early 1920s, his tutors "infected" him with a deep admiration for Lord Acton, and so he spent a great deal of time studying his papers stored at Cambridge University Library (CUL; where Acton's library and papers were housed after his death). His later attitude toward Acton, however, amounted to a diametrical reversal, bearing features of a love-hate feeling. On the one hand, he defended the study of Acton's writings, but, on the other, he felt the need to assault his legacy viciously.

In 1931, Butterfield published a little book titled *The Whig Interpretation of History*, in which he attacked a tendency among Whig historians to see the world as ethically progressing over time and achieving its pinnacle in the constitutional and representative regime. Consequently, English constitutional liberty sets a pattern for all humankind to follow and offers easy criteria for distinction between the friends and foes of progress and freedom. Butterfield also strongly rejected judging the past by present standards and interests, in particular by universal moral principles. Finally, he made it clear that Acton was his primary target. In his booklet he mentioned Acton nearly a hundred times, devoted an entire chapter to the critique of his idea of moral judgment, and ultimately cast him as the epitome of a Whig historian ("in Lord Acton, the Whig historian reached his highest consciousness").

The attack was clever and effective: by attacking old-fashioned historiography, the Whig perception of history as a linear progression, and moral judgments in history, he imputed to Acton guilt for all "transgressions" of anachronic and Whiggish history, even if he could be held accountable only for the last, that is, moral judgment of the past. In turn, Acton's call for objective, supranational history, the study of ideas, and the use of archival and primary sources, as well as his merits in transferring this new approach to England, fell into oblivion, while his image of a failed historian and an "unproductive monument" was revived. Butterfield knew the dominant trends in historiography and, more generally, the spirit of the time after World War I. By "boldly" assaulting the methods that had been already falling out of use, he made a name for himself in academia but maligned the name of the man whose thought he could not grasp.

About twenty-five years later, Butterfield again dismissed Acton as the "old-fashioned historian." By 1955, when these words were published, he was probably right. A historian's work inevitably ages and gradually turns old-fashioned, even if it becomes a classic. Acton the historian, however, did make a lasting impact on the way history is researched and written. In addition to his support for Ranke's methods and his own contribution to the methodology of history and their spread in England, he deserves recognition for his editorship of the *Cambridge Modern History* (*CMH*). Although he died before its first volume was printed, for the next ten years (1902–1912) Cambridge University Press (CUP) continued to publish the series according to his design. Even if still Eurocentric, the *CMH* was the first attempt to write the history of the West, one in which not national borders but long-term fundamental changes and the work of ideas played decisive roles. Good historians are still using this approach, extending it to world history.

As for the call for moral judgment, the idea has long been put to rest. Being a strict moralist, Acton wished to elevate history into a much more sublime plain than, in fact, it belongs. Remaking it into a moral tribunal was not his ultimate goal: he aimed still higher. As George P. Gooch, his younger friend at Cambridge, states, Acton wanted history to be "a school of virtue and a guide to life." In Acton own words, written in the report to the syndics of CUP, history was to be "not a burden on the memory but an illumination of the soul." Owen Chadwick reminds us that those who talked to Acton or listened to his lectures "felt that the wisdom of the ages was speaking through him," and concludes that "in a sense Acton was the poet of history." And this title—the *poet of history*—is probably the most suitable to render Acton's role in the field of history.

Acton's Legacy as a Political Thinker

Acton's thoughts on liberty were not fully grasped in the period shortly after his death. As mentioned in the previous section, early reviewers of his works found fault with his failure to write a history of liberty, noticed his emphasis on the intimate link between morality and politics, and wondered at his many paradoxical statements on liberty in history that often contradicted the Whiggish (and the Protestant) perspective of the past and yet were highly critical of the Catholic Church.

Perhaps the most mature view of Acton's teaching on freedom in the early period belonged to Herbert A. L. Fisher, an Oxford historian and liberal politician. He seems to be the first one who understood that Acton's warnings against equality and democracy did not make him an enemy of either. True, Acton saw "the essential incompatibility of liberty and equality" and democracy's great potential to devolve into tyranny. But he was also a great enthusiast of the American (undoubtedly democratic) Constitution with its checks and balances and federalist structure; furthermore, his warnings about democracy were conditional: democracy is a menace to liberty only if it lacks the safeguards provided by a "multiplicity of checking forces," such as the church, the nobility, and other intermediate institutions. Fisher applied this teaching to the past, in particular to the French Revolution, because in 1920 when his book was published the democratic potential for tyranny was not easily foreseeable.

Acton's thoughts on politics and liberty gradually fell into oblivion in the interwar period, especially after Butterfield's onslaught on his legacy. He then appeared passé, not only as a historian but also as a political thinker. Benefiting from a long tradition of representative government, legal equality, and individual rights, the West seemed secure from tyranny and looked as if it had no need of Acton's warnings about the perils of democracy (his habitual term for mass politics based on equality). Furthermore, the West's sense of superiority blinded it to the lessons Bolshevik despotism was teaching, particularly that Soviet Russia rationalized its atrocities with slogans about equality and social and economic justice. Consequently, the rediscovery of Acton occurred only after Europe's experience with German totalitarianism and the cataclysm of World War II: the generation who had lived through it was much more open to warnings about the side effects of "democracy."

Since World War II, America has been the site of the revival of Acton study. This was spearheaded by émigrés from Austria and Germany and from continental Europe more generally, especially Hayek, Karl Popper, and Isaiah Berlin. Considering Acton to be one of the greatest political thinkers of the nineteenth century, they all stimulated interest in him among a younger generation of scholars and the wider public. Hayek deserves special attention in this respect because he made extensive use of Acton's ideas and incorporated them into his concept of liberalism, which was strikingly similar to Acton's own.

In his famous book *The Road to Serfdom*, written during the war, Hayek put Acton on a par with Tocqueville and praised Acton for his defense of individual liberty and objection to the centralization of power and rationalistic formulas. In a paper presented at King's College at the University of Cambridge (1944), he pointed out that Acton could uniquely serve Allied efforts to reeducate the Germans. Because he was viewed as one of their own (Acton was half-German by birth), many would be attracted to his political teachings on liberty, including his call for moral judgment of the past: "The future historian must have the courage to say that Hitler was a bad man." Furthermore, Hayek adds, "What the Germans need . . . is a strong dose of what it is now the fashion to call 'Whig history,' history of the kind of which Lord Acton is one of the last great representatives." Hayek had none of Butterfield's prejudice against the Whigs. On the contrary, he made Whiggism essential in his own concept of genuine liberalism. Thus, describing Acton as a Whig historian was meant favorably, not unfavorably.

Hayek distinguishes between two kinds of rationalism in the Western tradition: the "constructivist" version, which is given "to building magnificent philosophical systems," and a "more modest and less ambitious" one, which, despite its limited aims, achieved much more than the first by laying "the foundation of modern European civilization and particularly the political order of liberalism." Among its greatest modern figures, he lists Montesquieu, Hume, and Adam Smith as well as Tocqueville, Acton, and, more recently, thinkers of the Austrian School of Economics (to which Hayek himself belonged). The roots of the more ambitious constructivist school lie in Descartes and French rationalism and it found its extreme expression in Hegel and Marx, although even some German liberals—such as Kant and Alexander von Humboldt—and the English utilitarians "did not wholly escape the fatal attraction of Rousseau and French rationalism."

Hayek's general perspective on Western political thought sets a convenient background for understanding his notion of two currents within liberalism, a notion that is nearly identical to Acton's. Like Acton, Hayek links one of its currents with the tradition much older than the term itself, that is, classical antiquity and its modern form, which developed "during the late seventeenth and the eighteenth centuries as the political doctrine of the English Whigs. It was the individual liberty which a 'government under the law' had secured to the citizens of Great Britain." He brands this liberalism "evolutionary." The second current interpreted English institutions in light of a "rationalist or constructivistic view," predominant in the continental philosophical tradition, which "demanded a deliberate reconstruction of the whole of society in accordance with principles of reason." This current, dubbed constructivist or continental liberalism, gained great influence in the eighteenth century through the *philosophes* of the Enlightenment and dominated during the French Revolution. "The core of this movement . . . was not so much a definite political doctrine as a general mental attitude, a demand for an emancipation from all prejudice and all beliefs which could not be rationally justified, and for an escape from the authority of 'priests and kings.'"

Hayek's view of liberalism, its origins, and its two currents—one genuine and evolutionary, the other constructivist and continental ("which has always and everywhere been profoundly antiliberal")—is much more complex than the sketch just presented. But even this brief summary shows either the strong influence of Acton's thought on Hayek or at least a strong correspondence between their outlooks. At any rate, Acton had an impact, directly or indirectly, on a new political and economic current of liberalism that after World War II began to be called neoliberalism. In view of Acton's contempt for the Tories and conservatism, it seems paradoxical, but he may have had a similar impact on neoconservatism as well.

The increased interest in Acton after the war also produced new attempts by a younger generation of scholars to evaluate his life and legacy. Gertrude Himmelfarb's *Lord Acton: A Study in Conscience and Politics* (1952) was probably the most important among them. She made extensive use of Acton's notes stored in CUL, and on that basis, as well as a detailed review of his published works, she produced his intellectual biography. Her monograph presents Acton's pursuits and passions chronologically, beginning with his education and editorship of Catholic journals, reviewing his quarrels with the Catholic Church, his ambivalent attitude toward Edmund Burke, his support for the South in the American Civil War, and his condemnation of nationalism, and ending with his unwritten history of liberty, the call for moral evaluation of the past, and his last years at the University of Cambridge.

Probably alluding to Acton's complaints that he had "never had any contemporaries," Himmelfarb states in her book's opening paragraph that Acton "is of this age, more than of his. He is, indeed, one of our great contemporaries." A few pages later, she even calls him "a prophet of our time." These words characterize her book as an attempt to reread Acton in the post-Nazi period and apply his thought in the era of Western rivalry with Soviet communism. Meticulously researched, her book became a classic on Acton's thought and remains so to this day. Himmelfarb, the wife of the neoconservative intellectual Irving Kristol, doubtless contributed to the popularity of Acton's critical view of doctrinaire liberalism among neoconservatives.

Himmelfarb was not alone in calling Acton a prophet for the World War II generation. Others also noted that "in essay after essay he [had] prophesied the horrors that would afflict the twentieth century" and emphasized his defense of genuine liberalism. In this context, they bestowed on him the title of "a prophet of liberalism," one of "the oracles of Liberal faith," or "a minor prophet of political theory."

Not all reviewers of Acton's life and thought were equally enthusiastic in the postwar period. Lionel Kochan in his monograph *Acton on History* (1954) asserts that Acton lacked intellectual courage. He displayed it as the editor of Catholic journals, as a deputy in the House of Commons, as an opponent of papal infallibility, and as the proponent of morality in historiography. Each time, however, he acquiesced under the pressures of his environment, preferring to withdraw and keep silent instead of fighting for his own views. The unwritten history of liberty is another example of his compromises with an unfriendly intellectual milieu. Kochan's book rivals Himmelfarb's in the meticulousness of the research and uses the same chronological approach in serially analyzing Acton's various works. Both use Acton's notes extensively, although—as Hill rightly states—notes unsupported by other evidence are of dubious value because no one knows if they express Acton's views or someone else's. Further, neither book tries to capture the essence of Acton's teachings on liberty that would transcend messages in his individual works.

In the 1960s, two monographs are worth mentioning, one written by Josef L. Altholz and the other by David Mathew. The focus of the first, *The Liberal Catholic Movement in England: The "Rambler" and Its Contributors, 1848–1864*, is the liberal Catholic movement in England and, specifically, the important role in it played by the *Rambler* and the *Home and Foreign Review*. As such, it provides detailed research on Acton's work as the editor of these journals (1858–1864) and the part he played in the demise of liberal Catholicism. Altholz concludes, "Too liberal to submit [to church hierarchy], too Catholic to secede, the Liberal Catholics rested their hopes in posterity, which has by and large ignored them."

The second monograph, *Lord Acton and His Time*, written by a British Catholic bishop and historian, presents Acton's life against the background of two worlds, the Victorian and the Catholic. This book, the second Mathew wrote on Acton (the first was devoted to his youth), is a solid biography, still interesting, especially since its author often takes the perspective of Catholic hierarchy. That is, Mathew views Acton from an angle not typical for his biographers. For example, commenting on his visit to America, Mathew says that in his youth Acton had an odd habit of "call[ing] on Catholic bishops who were strangers to him, to hobnob with them and to cross-examine"; or, presenting Acton's audiences with Pius IX, Mathew sides not with the subject of his biography but with the pope—again, an unlikely perspective for an Acton biographer.

Robert L. Schuettinger's *Lord Acton: Historian of Liberty* is the last work that could be linked to the postwar increase of interest in Acton. It was published long after the war (1976) but rooted in the place directly linked to the postwar revival of Actonian studies: the University of Chicago and its Committee on Social Thought. Hayek worked there and inspired Schuettinger's interest in Acton. The author stresses his indebtedness to Himmelfarb's monograph and, in this expression of debt, he is sincere: he follows her approach but brings little new in terms of evidence and interpretation.

In spite of the new wave of publishing and republishing of Acton's writing that began in the 1960s and continued until the 1980s, interest in his political thought gradually faded. Although something on various Acton's pursuits was published nearly every year in this period—in the form of either journal articles or introductions to collections of Acton's original writing—there appeared no serious attempt to evaluate his political thought until the end of the twentieth century. Owen Chadwick says that this was due to Acton's failure to publish more: writers are judged "by what they had published and not by the books that they owned or by the pile of facts that they were known to know. Acton had succeeded in publishing very little."

Chadwick's opinion seems unfair. As stated earlier, Acton did publish a lot—his publications can easily fill a solid bookshelf. He did not, however, publish a book and, no doubt, this is his fundamental weakness. Yet the diminished interest in his thought seems to have different causes. By the 1960s the memory of World War II and Nazi atrocities began to fade (while Soviet atrocities were never fully acknowledged in the West), and that is why he gradually ceased to be a "contemporary" and a prophet for people living in prosperous democracies. His teachings about the unwanted side effects of mass politics could no longer appeal to liberal Western societies. If he found followers curious about and excited by his teachings they lived in East-Central Europe, which was dominated by the Soviet Union.

In 2000, Roland Hill published the most comprehensive biography of Lord Acton so far. The book is the result of his in-depth research on Acton, shedding light on many previously unknown or little-known episodes of his public and personal life. Hill also discusses Acton's main writings on liberty but, as does Himmelfarb, he reviews each piece separately, one essay after another, without trying to reconcile inconsistences or synthesize his political teachings.

The most recent monograph on Acton, *Power Tends to Corrupt: Lord Acton's Study of Liberty* (2012), by the author of the present volume, takes a different approach. The book thoroughly examines Acton's writing in search of his understanding of liberty. By analyzing views scattered over many of Acton's essays, reviews, and letters and explaining contradictions in his pronouncements, it tries to arrange his thoughts into a coherent whole. It consequently recreates Acton's history of liberty, not the way he intended to write it (mining all available primary sources and the most recent scholarly publications) but the way he in fact left it, without bringing it all together in one piece. Furthermore, by searching for Acton's political principles and arranging them hierarchically, the book presents his theory of liberty as well.

The Not-So-Friendly, Even Hostile, Reception to Acton

In their introduction, the editors of *Lectures on Modern History* (1906) noted that "there has been in some quarters a tendency to belittle the activity of the late Professor, a tendency which indicates the same limited intellectual horizon as the denial that he was a historian." However, critical and, at times, hostile commentary on Acton's ideas and scholarly output did not follow his death but preceded it.

Acton's inaugural lecture at Cambridge received a very positive reception but also generated negative reactions. Some sarcastically suggested that Lord Acton was a living example of a historian who knew too much; others said he was pretentious, someone who, overwhelmed by his own "deluge of verbiage," did not even grasp what he was saying; still others were more specific in attacking his call for moral judgment of the past: a historian, "if he aspires to be a judge, . . . should not try a case by a code unknown to the defendant."

This argument, soon to become a constant accusation made against Acton the historian, was raised by the American historian Henry C. Lea. Roland Hill suspects ulterior motives in Lea's attack:

Acton had written a review of his *History of the Inquisition of the Middle Ages*, ostensibly complimenting it but really demolishing it, and now it was Lea's turn to take revenge. Hill judges it unfair, because Acton stressed that the moral code is not unknown but universal and familiar to all. Perhaps Lea's anti-Catholic bias also played a role in his assaults on Acton.

Some obituaries of Acton were equivocal as well. Owen Chadwick quotes *The Times*' obituary, which, after noting Acton's erudition and kindness, scored his mental timidity: "With greater moral courage and more sturdy literary conscience Lord Acton would have made a more striking mark in letters and in public affairs."

As mentioned, from the early 1930s the writings of Herbert Butterfield generated a negative reception of Acton's thought. As a historian, Acton has never regained the reputation he enjoyed late in his life and in the two decades after his death. Even as liberty's historian and passionate lover, he was often misunderstood or mocked. As we noted in the introduction, his teachings cannot be easily grasped, and those who ignore their complexity face many puzzles. For how can he claim to be liberal, yet mercilessly assail liberalism; support liberal economics, yet demand care for the poor; hate conservatism, yet side with the South in the American Civil War; admire Burke, but claim he ought to have been hanged; and extol the Catholic Church as the chief mainstay of liberty, yet condemn its hierarchy and wash its history's dirty laundry in public?

This list of paradoxes can be lengthened. It is therefore no wonder that some reviewers of Acton could misapprehend or dismiss him. As a result, some branded his stern morality as Kantian, even Pelagian (as if he confused what one ought to do with what one can do); others denied his liberalism and called him a socialist (because he defended the disadvantaged); still others treated him as "a partisan of the sinking ship" (because he sided with the

Southern Confederacy). There were also some who dismissed him as a phony thinker who repeatedly incanted "liberty" instead of explaining its meaning. For such critics, Acton was an "unproductive monument" who deserves only to be left to "honourable oblivion."

Recent Publications

The renewed interest in Acton's thought after World War II resulted in the publication of a series of new collections of his writings and the republishing of some old editions, usually accompanied by new introductions presenting his life and legacy. These publications can be organized into three groups. The first comprises collections of correspondence. Of these, two collections deserve special attention: the first, with Döllinger, was edited in Germany by Victor Conzemius (3 vols., 1963–1981); the second, with Richard Simpson, was edited by Josef L. Altholz, Damian McElrath, and James C. Holland (3 vols., 1971–1975). The second group of publications includes diaries and journals. In 1946, Butterfield edited Acton's notes from the trip he took to Rome with Döllinger. Another diary of Acton's, written during the Vatican Council and discovered posthumously, was published in 1975. A few years later, a journal from his trip to America, originally published in installments in the *Fortnightly Review* (1921–1922), was republished as a book. The third group consists of new publications of his essays and other writings, as well as a new edition of his lectures. These are *Essays on Freedom and Power* (edited by Gertrude Himmelfarb, 1948, 1955, and 1964 editions); *Essays on Church and State* (edited by Douglas Woodruff, 1952, 1953, and 1968 editions); *Essays in the Liberal Interpretation of History* (edited by William H. McNeill, 1967); and *Lord Acton: The Decisive Decade, 1864–1874: Essays and*

Documents (edited by Damian McElrath, 1970). Both *Lectures on Modern History* and *Lectures on the French Revolution* underwent several reprintings, some with new introductions or forewords. What is notable is that some of these publications were not only issued more than once but also made available on the internet, confirming continued public interest in Acton's writing.

Finally, there is a publication that deserves separate treatment: a three-volume selection of Acton's most important essays, reviews, and notes edited by the late Professor J. Rufus Fears and published by the Liberty Fund between 1985 and 1988 as *Selected Writings of Lord Acton*. The publication is generously endowed with an editor's foreword and a biographical sketch of Acton, as well as reviews of each volume's contents and bibliographical information. It is an indispensable compendium and guide through Acton's writing to anyone who cares to study his thought.

With this as well as with earlier publications, Acton's legacy has been nearly entirely made public. What has not yet been republished are many book reviews originally printed in the nineteenth-century journals that Acton edited or collaborated with. Most of his notes have never been published either, although Fears placed some of the most interesting notes in the third volume of his *Selected Writings*. The opportunity to study Acton has never been greater. Fears encourages this study by the striking remarks of his foreword written in 1984:

> Students of Acton have made much—too much, we might say—of his failure to write more for publication. The fact is that . . . Acton left an intellectual legacy of seminal importance. Drawing upon that legacy in the 1930's and 1940's, scholars . . . discovered an Acton who spoke with prophetic power to a generation witnessing the material and moral ruin of Europe and the triumph of state absolutism in the guise of fascist and communist regimes. Through these

> writings Acton remains our contemporary. . . . His insights into the nature of man and politics, into the meaning of human liberty, and into those forces which foster and which threaten human freedom ring more profoundly true than when he penned them more than a century ago. His message is one of supreme importance to every thoughtful citizen of a democratic society.

Roland Hill in his life of Acton seems to concur:

> Acton may have left little in the way of finished books or a system of ideas. His written work is nonetheless substantial and impressive. . . . Unlike other great Victorians, his influence has increased rather than diminished in the century following his death. His ideas and jottings, like Blaise Pascal's *Pensées* not ordered by the author himself, continue to attract attention because of their enigmatic character. The very failures of his own life's struggles seem lessons to be learned from one of humanity's great teachers of freedom. Perhaps after the horrors of Auschwitz and the Gulag we feel that they might have been lessened if in his own and subsequent time more attention had been paid to freedom as the moral and religious end of society.

These two quotes by two recognized authorities on Lord Acton's life and thought—J. Rufus Fears and Roland Hill—express better than anything the idea that Acton's thought is still worthy of studying and contemplating. The only addition that comes to mind is that Acton did not only warn us about the threat of brutal dictatorship, such as Nazism and communism. No, he seemed to warn us equally about the tragic potential of (il)liberal democracy and the modern state. Such a regime, ostensibly caring about the common good and universal comfort, has no less potential to turn into a dreadful tyranny, and like the Rousseauian "general will" could force us to be "free" as defined by a totalitarian democracy.

Conclusion

Acton's Lessons for Today

Having titled this book *Lord Acton for Our Time*, we will now check the bold claim it implies against the book's contents. We will begin with simple inferences and then move on to issues of greater gravity.

Acton's writings offer us an opportunity to benefit from his extraordinary erudition. Who among today's readers has the time and determination to read as many books as he did, both primary and secondary sources? Granted, reading his writings requires an effort to learn his language, but the effort pays off, for it opens the gate to his many original ideas and concepts, challenging views of our own that we once assumed to be unshakable. His thought lets us not only revise our preconceptions about the past but also provides comparative materials for reflecting on the problems and dilemmas of our time. A few examples will illustrate how Acton provides such food for thought.

First, one of the fundamental missions of Christianity, especially the Catholic Church, was to limit state power and ensure religious liberty for the individual and the faithful, and autonomy for the church, thus making religious freedom the first human right, beyond the purview of the state. According to Acton, the Catholic Church fulfilled that mission in antiquity and in the Middle Ages but betrayed it utterly in the early modern period. The Reformation, born of protest against the corruption of the church, did not increase liberty, however. On the contrary, by subordinating the church to the state and giving rulers the right to impose their faith on their subjects, it paved the way to absolutism, which Acton brands "a studied philosophy of crime." If this claim is true, ought we not ask what will happen to us if we remove religion and its churches entirely from the public square? Will we gain greater freedom, or undermine the freedom we have by removing such a mighty bastion against state interference in one of the most intimate spheres of our lives?

Second, according to Acton, the "rights of man"—civil and political rights, or basic human rights—have medieval roots and arose from the struggle between the papacy and the empire, and more generally between church and state. Another phase of this conflict took place in the religious wars of the sixteenth and seventeenth centuries. Ideas and principles of freedom, individual and corporate, that were born or reborn during these wars were taken over by nascent liberalism after those notions had shed their religious roots and acquired a secular form. If Acton is right about this genealogy, liberalism in fact has religious roots. The anti-religious bias of constructivist liberalism seems to be a struggle against its own foundation; it substitutes ideology for religion but preserves its zeal.

Third, if Acton is right, the French Revolution did not usher in the principle of popular sovereignty, thereby inaugurating the liberal age, because the principle that power comes from the people had been established in the West from time immemorial. All the Revolution did in this regard was to redefine "people" and "nation" and impose doctrinaire liberalism on continental Europe, which had dire consequences for civic liberty. From Acton's perspective, it was the Glorious Revolution and the American Revolution (i.e., not real revolutions) that truly gave wing to mature liberty and became the cornerstones of the liberal order in the Anglo-American world.

Fourth, liberty requires citizens, the organic growth of their political institutions, and the acknowledgment of natural law as the only rules independent of human will. This breeds genuine liberalism according to Acton, whereas invoking abstract principles and trimming life to fit doctrine leads to a phony liberalism that is in fact illiberal. If so, then he inspires us to ask whether the period after the French Revolution was truly a liberal age for the West, as we commonly believe, or whether it was merely another version of the old rule of the strongest but hidden behind a veil of lofty slogans. This, in turn, may prompt a more urgent question: Does the liberal order of the twenty-first century provide us with a life in freedom, or only an illusion of it, such as is dramatically imagined in *The Matrix*?

Fifth, Acton stresses the supreme importance of higher, natural law as the only arbitrary element in political life. As stated, the rest is shaped by a slow evolution of political regime that deals with daily challenges step by step without resorting to wholesale schemes and revolutionary means. But can we profit from these rules if we reject not only the notion of natural law but also nature itself? If all is fluid, one of the bedrocks on which ordered liberty rests disappears. Can liberal democracy survive it and still secure freedom for us?

Let us now move on to Acton's theory of liberty and his version of liberalism, issues of fundamental importance to anyone who wants to live in freedom. He made liberty the supreme principle in politics and rejected any other precept contending for that exalted place. And yet, putting liberty in such an elevated position did not mean that it could be capricious or willful. He disagreed with those who conceived of liberty as the right to do what one would like, even if limited by the equal right of others to do likewise, as colloquial liberalism counsels. No, he surrounded liberty with a set of complementary principles that circumscribe it and give it its proper meaning and scope and make it truly an ordered liberty.

In brief, liberty is the freedom to do what we ought to do both as individuals and as citizens. This "ought" (duty) has two aspects, moral and civic. Liberty is thus limited, first by the dictates of our conscience and morality formed by natural law and second by the traditions, laws, and customs of our communities. The former has an individual dimension, the latter a communal dimension; both are of equal importance. Consequently, we again see that in the Actonian concept of civic liberty (and his organic liberalism) there is no place for inherent conflict between individuals and their polity, an insoluble quandary for constructivist liberalism. On the contrary, as citizens, individuals are firmly embedded in their community; it is they who shape it as they are shaped by it.

Acton's theory also emphasizes that liberty is an end, not a state of being, and that it evolves to meet the many challenges that life brings. In other words, freedom has a history and therefore a tradition that is essential to its organic development. Like a tree or a language, liberty grows by itself and does not need sophisticated designs or social engineering (features typical of constructivist liberalism). It is as if a polity develops toward a more advanced liberty by an invisible hand.

What is needed to start such a course—and animate the invisible hand of liberty—is a seed of freedom at the moment of the polity's foundation. Acton does not elaborate what that embryonic form must contain, but we can infer that it must acknowledge popular sovereignty, show awareness of a higher law, and respect the emerging tradition, just as in the Hebrew notion of liberty. For a new polity, this initiates a process of growing toward more mature freedom. It is a long and arduous journey, full of obstacles, failures, and setbacks. However, by gradually eliminating legal inequality, admitting new groups to citizenship, and becoming more sensitive to injustice, while respecting tradition and higher law, it leads toward more advanced civic as well as civil freedom.

Acton had no doubt that liberty cannot be established by an assault on the community and its tradition. Revolution is "a malady, a frenzy," a painful wound that cannot produce a liberal order on demand. At best, it might initiate a new regime that will begin its long path toward ordered freedom, but it usually proves fatal, either evolving into an arbitrary form of power or threatening the state's existence or independence.

Another key feature of Acton's theory of liberty is self-governance. Order that fosters freedom is born from below, in a community in which people solve their own problems. Such circumstances create citizens, that is, individuals who take their lives into their hands. (Acton scorned "citizens" who obtain their voting and civil rights by central government fiat, not their own action.) In such an order, higher levels of power emanate from lower levels, not the other way around, and each retains its authority in its own sphere. The old Catholic principle of subsidiarity ought to be maintained throughout the entire structure of government: problems are to be addressed at the lowest level of power that has the means and the right to solve them. Consequently, Acton envisioned power as a set of concentric circles, from the lowest (city and county) to the highest (national), each acting in its own sphere and respecting the prerogatives of others.

The liberty of the moderns, unlike that of the ancients, includes freedom *from* politics. Representative and divided government as well as widespread franchise released us from the duty to be involved in politics the way the ancient Greeks had to be engaged in it and gave us the luxury of a private life. However, keeping in mind Acton's thought about the intimate links between liberty, self-government, morality, and true citizens, ought we not ask whether we, like Athenian *idiotai*, have gone too far in elevating private life at the expense of the public sphere, which we have left to the bureaucracy and its services? Will we not end up like the ancients in Rome, with an all-powerful state on the one hand and rights devoid of substance on the other?

These questions, weighty enough in themselves, acquire greater gravity in light of Acton's remarks on the inherent flaws of democracy and the drift of the modern state toward arbitrary power, a drift that could end in it having total control of society. To put this in context, let us remember that he was not against democracy and the state as such but against their deviations. He viewed popular sovereignty as the only legitimate form of government and supported the broadest suffrage possible under the circumstances. He also considered the state an essential good, not a necessary evil, as constructivist liberalism tends to believe. He did not, however, worship democracy—a tendency common in our own age—and he was truly scared of the growth of modern state.

Democracy has the potential to be the best regime if properly contained and balanced. Acton's idea of national liberty—his best practical regime—seems to be a such a comprehensively balanced and limited democracy. This is but one element of his theory, however. Another equally important element is that people must remain vigilant because of the inherent limitations and flaws of this form of government. We have little or no shield against democracy's penchant for "unity of power," its intolerance of what is beyond mainstream opinion, its disregard for tradition, merit, and decency, and finally its susceptibility to manipulation and rapid changes of mood. It is as if Acton is telling us that distrust of democracy is, paradoxically, a constitutive element of a healthy democracy. Consequently, we can ask, do we have such a prudent attitude toward democracy, or do we tend to idolize it, as if it were an end in itself, rather than a means to an end?

This warning is urgent given the potential of democracy for degeneration. If the flaws of an insufficiently balanced and checked democracy grow unimpeded, it can evolve not only into the most lenient of bad regimes, as Aristotle argued, but also into the worst, even into an unimaginable nightmare. This may occur when a deviated democracy meets the modern state. Both strongly incline to centralization and uniformity and share a disregard for secondary authorities. When Acton cautioned against the amalgamation of pure democracy, the modern state, and revolutionary measures, he showed that he grasped what totalitarianism is, even if he did not call it by that name. Thoughtful people who had lived through communist and Nazi tyrannies comprehended his warnings, and that is why they considered him the prophet of their generation.

More difficult to discern is the development of a "soft" version of this despotism, originally an agency of utilitarianism and doctrinaire liberalism, which expresses the will of the people (or what pretends to be such), cares for their well-being (sparing them "the trouble of thinking and all the pain of living"), and grants the government both omnipresence and omnipotence as it pursues its tasks. If this is combined with contempt for tradition and the rights of intermediary bodies, as well as timidity in the face of the vagaries of popular mood and street violence, then it might end up as another version of the old nightmare. It could have sprung from the noblest of intentions and assumed the loftiest of goals but, in the end, it will be no less vicious and ruthless than "hard-core" totalitarianism.

Acton warns that oppression dressed up as the democratic will is more pervasive and leaves fewer options for escape than oppression by a tyrant or the despotism of a group. "From the absolute will of an entire people there is no appeal, no redemption, no refuge but treason."

AFTER WORLD WAR II, Acton was proclaimed the prophet for that time—regrettably, however, only after the fact. Will we be wise enough to honor him as one of the prophets for our time before the worst befalls us? Will we find the courage to counter current trends by reversing democratic deviation and state corruption before a new species of tyranny engulfs us?

It depends on us, not Acton, whether we find that courage and demonstrate that wisdom. But whatever the outcome of our parlous state, Acton has an optimistic message for us: liberty can never be completely eradicated; it finds its own way to escape the perils that threaten to snuff it out. It may take unexpected forms, but freedom always regenerates and, phoenix-like, rises from the ashes. And when favorable conditions obtain, it blossoms anew.

Notes

1. A Brief Biography

p. 12 *Lord Acton's full name* This account of Acton's biography is based mainly on the most comprehensive and recent account of his life, Roland Hill's *Lord Acton* (New Haven, CT: Yale University Press, 2000).

p. 13 *"continental gentleman"* Hill quoting Queen Victoria's journal (*Lord Acton*, 15). See Herbert Fisher, *Studies in History and Politics* (Oxford: Clarendon Press, 1920), 86–87.

p. 13 *"the English boarding school"* Hill quoting Acton's letter dated December 8, 1842 (*Lord Acton*, 20).

p. 13 *The Count and Countess* Hill, *Lord Acton*, 6–15, 40–45.

p. 13 *His upbringing probably* James Bryce, *Studies in Contemporary Biography* (London and New York: Macmillan, 1903), 390; Mountstuart E. Grant Duff, *Out of the Past*, 2 vols. (London: John Murray, 1903), 2:123, 188; Owen Chadwick, *Acton and Gladstone* (London: Athlone Press, 1976), 8–10; Owen Chadwick, *Acton and History* (Cambridge: Cambridge University Press, 2002), 142–45.

p. 14 *He always thought he* Bryce, *Studies in Contemporary Biography*, 396.

p. 14 *These three—Döllinger* Hill, *Lord Acton*, 30–35, 59; Christopher Lazarski, *Power Tends to Corrupt: Lord Acton's Study of Liberty* (DeKalb, IL: Northern Illinois University Press, 2012), 5–6.

p. 15 *Despite the decreased* Hill, *Lord Acton*, 51–54.

p. 15 *Although this did not* Hill, *Lord Acton*, 33–35, 72–77.

p. 16 *"they pay 80 dollars"* [Lord Acton], "Lord Acton's American Diaries," *Fortnightly Review* (1921–1922), reprinted as *Acton in America: The American Journal of Sir John Acton, 1853*, ed. S. W. Jackman (Shepherdstown, WV: Patmos Press, 1979), 13, 16–18, 54.

p. 16 *This gave him occasion* Lord Acton to Ignaz von Döllinger, September 6, 1853, in *Ignaz von Döllinger Briefwechsel, 1820–1890*, ed. Victor Conzemius,

3 vols. (Munich: Bayerischen Akademie der Wissenschaften, 1963–1981), 1:38, hereafter referred to as *Briefwechsel.*

p. 16 *"My ideas will be"* Lord Acton to Ignaz von Döllinger, June 22, 1853, in *Briefwechsel*, 1:27–29.

p. 17 *He left no Russian* Hill, *Lord Acton*, 67–70.

p. 18 *When he visited* Hill, *Lord Acton*, 81–85.

p. 18 *Gladstone's Anglicanism did* Hill, *Lord Acton*, 86–92.

p. 19 *His reluctance to* Hill, *Lord Acton*, 92, 94–95, 192–93.

p. 19 *Their wedding took* Hill, *Lord Acton*, 157–62; see Chadwick, *Acton and Gladstone*, 7.

p. 20 *Their youngest, Jeanne* Hill, *Lord Acton*, 165–69.

p. 20 *We do not know* Hill, *Lord Acton*, 166–72, 281.

p. 20 *2nd Baron Acton* Hill, *Lord Acton*, 166–69.

p. 23 *Furthermore, the Catholic* Lord Acton, "Döllinger on the Temporal Power," *Rambler*, n.s., 6 (November 1861), reprinted in John Emerich Edward Dalberg Acton, *Selected Writings of Lord Acton*, ed. J. R. Fears, 3 vols. (Indianapolis: Liberty Classics, 1985–1988), vol. 3, hereafter referred to as *SWLA*.

p. 24 *Although Acton admitted* Lord Acton, "The Protestant Theory of Persecution," *Rambler*, n.s., 6 (March 1862), reprinted in *SWLA*, vol. 2.

p. 25 *"combine the obedience"* Lord Acton, "Conflicts with Rome," *Home and Foreign Review* 4 (April 1864), reprinted in *SWLA*, 3:257.

p. 25 *Although both* Hill, *Lord Acton*, 155.

p. 26 *The council was to* "Vatican Council: The Question of Papal Infallibility," *New Advent: Catholic Encyclopedia*, accessed August 5, 2019, http://www.newadvent.org/cathen/15303a.htm.

p. 27 *The letters—most of* Lazarski, *Power Tends to Corrupt*, 280n35.

p. 27 *Finally, because infallibility* Hill, *Lord Acton*, 194–204, 212–25.

p. 27 *"stood alone against"* Hill, *Lord Acton*, 223–25; "The Question of Papal Infallibility."

p. 28 *He also provided* Lord Acton, letters to the editor of *The Times*, November 8, 1874, reprinted in *SWLA*, 3:363–67.

p. 28 *In response, he* Acton, letters to the editor of *The Times*, November 21, 29, December 9, 1874, reprinted in *SWLA*, 3:367–84.

p. 29 *Acton clarified the* Hill, *Lord Acton*, 261–67; Chadwick, *Acton and History*, 125–26.

p. 29 *On the contrary, with* Hill, *Lord Acton*, 373–74.

p. 29 *Ultimately, he sympathized* Thomas A. Howard, "A Question of Conscience: The Excommunication of Ignaz von Döllinger," *Commonweal*, September 29, 2014, https://www.commonwealmagazine.org/question-conscience. I owe this reference to Anthony Flood, a New York City writer and political thinker (and also a great proofreader: http://AnthonyGFlood.com).

p. 30 *By his prediction* Hill, *Lord Acton*, 273–75.

p. 30 *His review of Thomas* Both lectures were delivered to the members of the Bridgnorth Institution at the Agricultural Hall on February 26 and May 28, 1877 (hereafter referred to as "Freedom in Antiquity" and "Freedom in Christianity"), reprinted in *SWLA*, vol. 1. Lord Acton, "Sir Erskine May's *Democracy in Europe*," *Quarterly Review* 145 (January 1878), reprinted in *SWLA*, vol. 1, hereafter referred to as "Sir Erskine." See Bryce, *Studies in Contemporary Biography*, 396.

p. 31 *"I have never heard from"* Bryce, *Studies in Contemporary Biography*, 396–97.

p. 31 *"the greatest book that"* Hill, *Lord Acton*, 276; Mary Drew, *Acton, Gladstone and Others*, 2nd ed. (Port Washington, NY: Kennikat Press, 1968), 7–10.

p. 31 *To understand the reasons* See Lionel Kochan, *Acton on History* (London: Andre Deutsch, 1954), 31–33; Chadwick, *Acton and Gladstone*, 22.

p. 32 *"The more he read"* See Bryce, *Studies in Contemporary Biography*, 392, 396; Gertrude Himmelfarb, *Lord Acton: A Study in Conscience and Politics* (Chicago: University of Chicago Press, 1962), 145; Gertrude Himmelfarb, "Introduction," in John Emerich Edward Dalberg Acton, *Essays on Freedom and Power*, ed. Gertrude Himmelfarb, 2nd ed. (New York: Meridian Books, 1955), 17–18; G. P. Gooch, *History and Historians in the Nineteenth Century* (Boston: Beacon Press, 1959), 358. See Herbert Butterfield, *Man on His Past*, 1st ed. 1955 (Cambridge: Cambridge University Press, 1979), 62–99; Josef L. Altholz, Damian McElrath, and James C. Holland, eds., *The Correspondence of Lord Acton and Richard Simpson*, 3 vols. (Cambridge: Cambridge University Press, 1971–1975), 1:xiv, hereafter referred to as *Acton-Simpson Correspondence*; George Watson, *Lord Acton's History of Liberty: A Study of His Library, with an Edited Text of His History of Liberty Notes* (Aldershot: Scolar Press, 1995), 47.

p. 32 *Aware that intellectual* Lord Acton, *Lectures on Modern History*, ed. Hugh Trevor-Roper, 3rd ed. (Cleveland and New York: Meridian Books, 1967), 38, 40; John Emerich Edward Dalberg Acton, *Lectures on the French Revolution*, ed. Neville Figgis and Reginald Vere Laurence (London: Macmillan, 1910), 92; Acton-Creighton Correspondence, April 5, 1887, Add. Mss. 6871, reprinted in *SWLA*, vol. 2; Add. Mss. 5403, 19–20.

p. 33 *He sold his library* Hill, *Lord Acton*, 62, 282–83, 287–90, 292.

p. 33 *Acton published less* Chadwick, *Acton and History*, 156–59; Himmelfarb, *Lord Acton*, 144–46; Robert L. Schuettinger, *Lord Acton: Historian of Liberty* (LaSalle, IL: Open Court, 1976), 127–29; Hill, *Lord Acton*, 273, 275–76.

p. 33 *The queen liked him* For maneuvers behind Acton's appointment, see Chadwick, *Acton and History*, 204–10; Hill, *Lord Acton*, 342–48, 365–68.

p. 34 *"It was in truth"* Hill, *Lord Acton*, xx; John Pollock, "Lord Acton at Cambridge," *Independent Review* 2 (April 1904): 366.

p. 34 *"would probably find on his"* John Neville Figgis and Reginald Vere Laurence, "Introduction: Lord Acton as a Professor," in *Lectures on Modern*

History, ed. John Neville Figgis and Reginald Vere Laurence (London: Macmillan, 1906), xiii.

p. 35 *He certainly breathed* Figgis and Laurence, "Lord Acton as a Professor," xiv. See Chadwick, *Acton and History*, 227–31; Hill, *Lord Acton*, 382–90.

p. 35 *Whether by an English* See Lord Acton's "Inaugural Lecture on the Study of History," in *Lectures on Modern History*, 31–34; Chadwick, *Acton and History*, 239–42; Hill, *Lord Acton*, 371–72, 392–97; Himmelfarb, *Lord Acton*, 223–25.

p. 36 *A vast correspondence* Chadwick, *Acton and History*, 240–42; Hill, *Lord Acton*, 400–401. See G. N. Clark, "The Origin of the *Cambridge Modern History*," *Cambridge Historical Journal* 8 (1945); Josef L. Altholz, "Lord Acton and the Plan of the Cambridge Modern History," *Historical Journal* 39, no. 3 (September 1996).

p. 36 *He died on June 20* Hill, *Lord Acton*, 400–402, 498n40. Schuettinger quotes Acton's colleague Professor Frederick Maitland, who wrote, "It is paralysis; one arm and one leg useless, but mind unaffected." *Lord Acton*, 179.

2. The Theory of Liberty and Organic Liberalism

p. 38 *"liberty is not a means"* "Freedom in Antiquity," 22.

p. 39 *"the end of government" Lectures on the French Revolution*, 33.

p. 39 *All those aims* See Lord Acton, "The Revolution in Italy," *Rambler*, n.s., 3 (July 1860), reprinted in *SWLA*, 1:496–98; Lord Acton, "The Piedmontese Ultimatum to the Holy See," *Rambler*, n.s., 6 (January 1862), reprinted in *SWLA*, 1:462–63; Lord Acton, "Cavour," *Rambler*, n.s., 5 (July 1861), reprinted in *SWLA*, 1:441; Lord Acton, "Nationality," *Home and Foreign Review* 1, no. 1 (July 1862), reprinted in *SWLA*, 1:424; "Sir Erskine," 83.

p. 39 *"Liberty is a plant"* Lord Acton, "Colonies," *Rambler*, n.s., 6 (March 1862), reprinted in *SWLA*, 1:182; Lord Acton, "Emancipation of the Serfs in Russia," *Rambler*, n.s., 3 (July 1860), reprinted in *SWLA*, 1:505. In "Venn's Life of St. Francis Xavier," *Home and Foreign Review* 2, no. 3 (January 1863): 188, Acton adds, "[Liberty] is the highest fruit of political cultivation, and the rare reward of political virtue. But it requires innumerable conditions which did not exist [in premodern times]."

p. 39 *"The example of the Hebrew"* "Freedom in Antiquity," 8.

p. 40 *Acton appreciated* "Freedom in Antiquity," 7–8; "Sir Erskine," 57–58.

p. 40 *"It is not conceivable"* Lord Acton, "Mr. Goldwin Smith's *Irish History*," *Rambler*, n.s., 6 (January 1862), reprinted in *SWLA*, 2:76.

p. 41 *He abhorred* Acton argues this when discussing two currents among the early Whigs: Lord Acton, "Review of Thomas Arnold's *Manual of English Literature*," *Home and Foreign Review* 2, no. 3 (January 1863), reprinted in *SWLA*, 1:145; Lord Acton, "Review of Frederick Arnold's *Public Life of Lord Macaulay*,"

Home and Foreign Review 2, no. 3 (January 1863), reprinted in *SWLA*, 1:153; *Lectures on the French Revolution*, 29. See also "Freedom in Antiquity," 12; Lazarski, *Power Tends to Corrupt*, 121–22, 233.

p. 41 *Of divine origins* This is evidenced by his enthusiasm about the US Constitution and approval of the French Declaration of the Rights of Man and of the Citizen: *Lectures on Modern History*, 295; Lord Acton to Lady Blennerhassett, April 22, 1887, in *Selections from the Correspondence of the First Lord Acton*, ed. John Neville Figgis and Reginald Vere Laurence (London: Longmans, Green, 1917), 272–73, hereafter referred to as *Selections from the Correspondence*; *Lectures on the French Revolution*, 37, 106; Lord Acton, "The Civil War in America: Its Place in History," *Bridgnorth Journal*, January 20, 1866, reprinted in *SWLA*, 1:264, hereafter referred to as "Civil War in America."

p. 41 *National tradition* See p. 41 *He abhorred.*

p. 41 *"the point at which"* Quotations are from "The Revolution in Italy," 497; "Venn's Life of St. Francis Xavier," 188; "Mr. Goldwin Smith's *Irish History*," 85; Add. Mss. 4870, 28; "Protestant Theory of Persecution," 99.

p. 42 *The American Revolution* See "Colonies," 178–85; *Lectures on Modern History*, 25, 191–92, 290–95; *Lectures on the French Revolution*, 21; "Sir Erskine," 72–73; "Civil War in America," 264.

p. 42 *It is so not only* See Lord Acton, "The Roman Question," *Rambler*, n.s., 2 (January 1860): 146; "The Revolution in Italy," 496–98; "Cavour," 441; Lord Acton, "Notes on the Present State of Austria," *Rambler*, n.s., 4 (January 1861), reprinted in John Emerich Edward Dalberg Acton, *Essays on Church and State*, ed. Douglas Woodruff (London: Hollis and Carter, 1952), 345; "The Piedmontese Ultimatum to the Holy See," 462–63; "Nationality," 424; "Sir Erskine," 83; Lazarski, *Power Tends to Corrupt*, 230, 236.

p. 43 *"By liberty I mean" Lectures on the French Revolution*, 33; "Freedom in Antiquity," 7.

p. 43 *"the power of doing"* "The Roman Question," 146. Acton calls it "the Catholic notion of liberty," but he fully identifies himself with it within the same paragraph.

p. 44 *"The proper name" Lectures on Modern History*, 42, 25, 43, 193; see also 28. *Lectures on the French Revolution*, 227. Acton's understanding of freedom of conscience is not entirely Catholic.

p. 44 *Figure 1 graphically* See Christopher Lazarski, "Lord Acton's 'Organic' Liberalism and His Best Practical Regime," *Catholic Social Science Review* 25 (2020): 106.

p. 44 *"The moral law" Lectures on Modern History*, 40.

p. 45 *"The wisdom of divine"* Bryce, *Studies in Contemporary Biography*, 396; Add. Mss. 5648, 50; Add. Mss. 4991, 198; "Inaugural Lecture on the Study of History," *Lectures on Modern History*, 26–27; cf. "We have no thread through the enormous intricacy and complexity of modern politics except the idea of progress towards more perfect and assured freedom, and the divine right of free men," 194–95.

p. 46 *French provincial* "Freedom in Antiquity," 5–7.

p. 46 *"It is a delicate"* Add. Mss. 4991, 198; "Freedom in Antiquity," 5. See also "Venn's Life of St. Francis Xavier," 188.

p. 47 *The Glorious Revolution* Acton devoted three chapters (pp. 188–221) of his *Lectures on Modern History* to English history in the seventeenth century. See also Lord Acton, "J. G. Phillimore's *History of England during the Reign of George III*," *Home and Foreign Review* 3, no. 6 (October 1863): 713, reprinted in Lord Acton, *Historical Essays and Studies*, ed. John Neville Figgis and Reginald Vere Laurence (London: Macmillan, 1907), 403–4; "Freedom in Christianity," 47–49.

p. 47 *"liberty founded on equality" Lectures on the French Revolution*, 97.

p. 48 *"In this process" Lectures on Modern History*, 28, 207–8, 220–21; "Freedom in Christianity," 48–49.

p. 48 *"power, when it is"* "Colonies," 183–85; Lord Acton, "Political Causes of the American Revolution," *Rambler*, n.s., 5 (May 1861), reprinted in *SWLA*, 1:218–19, hereafter referred to as "Political Causes"; Add. Mss. 4938, 234.

p. 48 *"It is the one immortal" Lectures on the French Revolution*, 37; *Lectures on Modern History*, 295; "Civil War in America," 264.

p. 49 *He felt slavery Lectures on Modern History*, 295; "Civil War in America," 270, 274, 276–78; "Political Causes," 244–45, 251–59.

p. 49 *"A principle is always"* "Civil War in America," 276–77. This public lecture and "Political Causes," the first written after the war and the second at its beginning, are among Acton's most important writings on America and, naturally, on freedom. Between March 1861 and October 1863, he also authored reports on current events, originally published in the *Rambler* and continued in the *Home and Foreign Review*. They were reprinted as "Reports on the Civil War in America" in *SWLA*, vol. 1. See also *Lectures on Modern History*, 295; Lord Acton, "Review of Hudson's *Second War of Independence in America*," *Home and Foreign Review* 2 (April 1863), reprinted in *SWLA*, vol. 1. For Acton's complex attitude toward slavery and its impact on the American Civil War, see Himmelfarb, *Lord Acton*, 77–83; Lazarski, *Power Tends to Corrupt*, 161–67.

p. 51 *"The law of liberty"* Lord Acton to Mary Gladstone, December 14, 1880, and April 24, 1881, in Lord Acton, *Letters of Lord Acton to Mary, Daughter of the Right Hon. W. E. Gladstone*, ed. Herbert Paul, 2nd rev. ed. (London: Macmillan, 1913), 38, 72–74, hereafter referred to as *Letters of Lord Acton to Mary*; see also "Sir Erskine," 81; Add. Mss. 4945.

p. 51 *"This growing dominion" Lectures on Modern History*, 43; see also "Sir Erskine," 81; Add. Mss. 5399, 41.

p. 52 *He was, no doubt* Lord Acton to Lady Blennerhassett, February 1879, in *Selections from the Correspondence*, 54; Lord Acton to Mary Gladstone, December 18, 1884, in *Letters of Lord Acton to Mary*, 158–59; *Lecture on Modern History*, 27; Add. Mss. 4991, 198, and Add. Mss. 5011, 213.

p. 54 *"serve as a basis"* "Nationality," 411.

p. 54 *At this point Acton* "Cavour," 441–43; "Notes on the Present State of Austria," 345; "Mr. Goldwin Smith's *Irish History*," 75–76; Lord Acton, "Expectation of the French Revolution," *Rambler*, n.s., 5 (July 1861), reprinted in *SWLA*, 2:43–53; *Lectures on the French Revolution*, 5–19; 165, 199.

p. 55 *In this way, doctrinaire* "The Piedmontese Ultimatum to the Holy See," 462–63; "Notes on the Present State of Austria," 345; "Cavour," 441; "The Revolution in Italy," 496–98.

p. 55 *On the contrary, he branded* See "Nationality," 424; "Colonies," 180; "The Roman Question," 146.

p. 55 *In England, the term* Friedrich A. Hayek, *New Studies in Philosophy, Politics, Economics and the History of Ideas* (London: Routledge & Kegan Paul, 1982), 119–21. Cf. Guido de Ruggiero, *The History of European Liberalism*, trans. R. G. Collingwood (London: Oxford University Press, 1927), 93–135, 141–50; Eric Vögelin, "Liberalism and Its History," *Review of Politics* 36, no. 4 (October 1974): 506–7; Duncan Bell, "What Is Liberalism?" *Political Theory* 42, no. 6 (2014): 692–93 (Bell traces the term in England to the 1820s).

p. 56 *In a seminal essay* "Nationality," 409–33, especially 424–28; 432.

p. 56 *The rights of national* "Nationality," 425, 431–32. See Acton's approving remarks on John Calhoun's view of government in "Political Causes," 240–43.

p. 57 *Acton finds this* "Nationality," 425–29; 432.

p. 57 *Thus was modern* "Nationality," 417–22.

p. 58 *In the former* "Nationality," 422–24; 432–33. For more on Acton's view of nationalism, see Lazarski, *Power Tends to Corrupt*, 241–48.

p. 58 *"more absurd and more criminal"* "Nationality," 433. For Acton's view of socialism, see Lazarski, *Power Tends to Corrupt*, 249–51.

p. 60 *"people of Athens"* "Freedom in Antiquity," 12–14; "Political Causes," 216.

p. 60 *"Democracy tends to"* Lord Acton to Mary Gladstone, February 20, 1882, in *Letters of Lord Acton to Mary*, 98.

p. 61 *"The people is induced"* "Political Causes," 217; see also "Sir Erskine," 83.

p. 61 *"But from the absolute will"* "Freedom in Antiquity," 13.

p. 61 *"The . . . principle, that"* "Sir Erskine," 80.

p. 62 *Consequently, the parliamentary* "Sir Erskine," 83.

p. 62 *Federalism and other* Acton to Mary Gladstone, February 20, 1882, 98; "Freedom in Antiquity," 21; "Sir Erskine," 84. See also p. 48 *"It is the one immortal."*

p. 62 *"for the accomplishment"* "Colonies," 180.

p. 63 *"protected by the State"* "The Revolution in Italy," 497.

p. 63 *If they both* "Political Causes," 260; "Notes on the Present State of Austria," 345; "Colonies," 180; see also 236–37.

p. 63 *This new political nation* "Nationality," 427–28; 413–14.

p. 64 *"Under these circumstances"* "Notes on the Present State of Austria," 345.

p. 65 *"There is no mediator"* "Political Causes," 260.

p. 65 *That is why they* Himmelfarb, *Lord Acton*, vii; E. Drozdowski and H. Parker, "Lord Acton: A Prophet for This Generation?" *South Atlantic Quarterly* 3 (1953). See chapter 4 on Acton's legacy.

p. 66 *"the trouble of thinking"* Alexis de Tocqueville, *Democracy in America*, trans. and ed. Harvey C. Mansfield and Delba Winthrop (Chicago: University of Chicago Press, 2000), 663.

p. 66 *"If we do not bear"* Lord Acton, "Review of James Burton Robertson, *Lectures on Ancient and Modern History*," *Rambler*, n.s., 2 (March 1860), reprinted in *SWLA*, 3:515–16.

3. Acton's History of Liberty

p. 72 *All of this met* "Freedom in Antiquity," 8; "Sir Erskine," 57–58. See Lazarski, *Power Tends to Corrupt*, 38–39; Krzysztof Lazarski, "Liberty in Equality: Lord Acton's Teaching on Participatory Democracy," *Athenaeum* 63, no. 3 (2019): 13.

p. 72 *In the seventeenth* "Sir Erskine," 58; see Lazarski, *Power Tends to Corrupt*, 40.

p. 73 *Acton points to* "Freedom in Antiquity," 9–10; "Sir Erskine," 58–59. See Lazarski, *Power Tends to Corrupt*, 40–41.

p. 73 *This was the regime* "Freedom in Antiquity," 11–18; "Sir Erskine," 59–63; "Political Causes," 216. See Lazarski, *Power Tends to Corrupt*, 41–44.

p. 74 *The politai* (citizens) "Freedom in Antiquity," 17–18; Add. Mss. 5393, 17. See Benjamin Constant, *The Liberty of the Ancients Compared with That of Moderns* (1819), accessed April 5, 2021, https://oll.libertyfund.org/title/constant-the-liberty-of-ancients-compared-with-that-of-moderns-1819; Isaiah Berlin, "The Birth of Greek Individualism," in Henry Hardy (ed.), *Liberty* (Oxford: Oxford University Press, 2005), 287–321.

p. 75 *He preferred* "Freedom in Antiquity," 17–23; "Sir Erskine," 61–64; Add. Mss. 4870, 13; Add. Mss. 5586; Add. Mss. 5594, 80; Pollock, "Lord Acton at Cambridge," 377. See Lazarski, *Power Tends to Corrupt*, 47–52.

p. 75 *In turn, the absolute* "Freedom in Antiquity," 15–18, 23–25; "Freedom in Christianity," 30; "Sir Erskine," 64–68; Add. Mss. 4862, 39; Add. Mss. 5528, 155. See Lazarski, *Power Tends to Corrupt*, 44–47.

p. 76 *Beginning in AD 64* "Freedom in Antiquity," 17, 26–28; "Freedom in Christianity," 29–30; "Sir Erskine," 64–65; Lord Acton, "Political Thoughts on the Church," *Rambler*, n.s., 11 (January 1859), reprinted in *SWLA*, 3:31; "Mr. Goldwin Smith's *Irish History*," 83; Add. Mss. 5605, 47. See Himmelfarb, *Lord Acton*, 42, 135–37; Schuettinger, *Lord Acton*, 52; Lazarski, *Power Tends to Corrupt*, 52–54.

p. 77 *"Even in the fervent"* "Freedom in Christianity," 26–30; "Sir Erskine," 69; *Lectures on Modern History*, 25; "Political Thoughts on the Church," 22, 24–25. See Himmelfarb, *Lord Acton*, 42, 136–37; Kochan, *Acton on History*, 96–97; Lazarski, *Power Tends to Corrupt*, 52–55.

p. 77 *That tradition* "Freedom in Christianity," 30–33; "Sir Erskine," 69; Lazarski, *Power Tends to Corrupt*, 55.

p. 78 *Although originally* "Freedom in Christianity," 31; "Political Thoughts on the Church," 25–28.

p. 80 *"every baron"* "Freedom in Christianity," 31–33; "Sir Erskine," 69; "Nationality," 416–17; "Mr. Goldwin Smith's *Irish History*," 80. See Lazarski, *Power Tends to Corrupt*, 64–67.

p. 80 *"In this respect"* George H. Sabine, *A History of Political Theory*, 4th ed. (Hinsdale, IL: Dryden Press, 1973), 207.

p. 81 *Until then, popular* See "Freedom in Christianity," 32–33, 36–37; "Sir Erskine," 69–70; "Nationality," 412–14.

p. 81 *Third, since only* "Freedom in Christianity," 32; "Political Thoughts on the Church," 26–29; "Mr. Goldwin Smith's *Irish History*," 77–78; Lord Acton, "Hefele's Life of Ximenes," *Rambler*, n.s., 3 (July 1860), reprinted in *Essays on Church and State*.

p. 82 *"They differ . . . in"* "Mr. Goldwin Smith's *Irish History*," 77. See "Political Thoughts on the Church," 28; Lord Acton, "The Political System of the Popes," *Rambler*, n.s., 2 (January 1860), 3 (May 1860), and 4 (January 1861), reprinted in *Essays on Church and State*.

p. 82 *The Byzantine protection* Lord Acton, "The States of the Church," *Rambler*, n.s., 2 (March 1860), reprinted in *Essays on Church and State*.

p. 83 *Other European* "The States of the Church," 109–11; "The Political System of the Popes," 127–36.

p. 83 *Both sides sought* "Freedom in Christianity," 34. Lazarski, *Power Tends to Corrupt*, 70–76.

p. 84 *"The towns of Italy"* "Freedom in Christianity," 33.

p. 84 *In turn, his opponent* "Freedom in Christianity," 34, 35.

p. 85 *"The political produce"* "Freedom in Christianity," 36–37.

p. 86 *The new age Lectures on Modern History*, 19–20, 42, 82–83.

p. 86 *It is an agency* Lord Acton to Lady Blennerhassett, February 1879, in *Selections from the Correspondence*, 54–56; *Lectures on Modern History*, chapter III, "The Renaissance," 78–94. See Lazarski, *Power Tends to Corrupt*, 84–87.

p. 87 *There is only Lectures on Modern History*, 66–77. See Lazarski, *Power Tends to Corrupt*, 83–84, 89–90.

p. 87 *"As there is no such" Lectures on Modern History*, 87, 19, 59–60; "Freedom in Antiquity," 37; Add. Mss. 4976, 12; Add. Mss. 4982, 83. See Lazarski, *Power Tends to Corrupt*, 87–89.

p. 88 *"Possessing the power"* "Döllinger on the Temporal Power," 87; see "The Protestant Theory of Persecution," 101–12; *Lectures on Modern History*, 98–108.

p. 88 *Acton emphasizes that* "Freedom in Christianity," 38, 43–44; Lord Acton, "Review of Poirson's *Histoire du Règne de Henri IV*," *Dublin Review* 44 (March 1858), reprinted in *SWLA*, vol. 2. For more on Acton's view of the Reformation, see Lazarski, *Power Tends to Corrupt*, 90–93, 108–19.

p. 89 *The system had to* Lord Acton to Richard Simpson, January 5, 1862, in *Acton-Simpson Correspondence*, 2:251.

p. 89 *"a studied philosophy"* "Freedom in Christianity," 38. See Lazarski, *Power Tends to Corrupt*, 97–101.

p. 89 *"the combined efforts of the" Lectures on Modern History*, 60, 161; "Sir Erskine," 70–71; "Freedom in Christianity," 41.

p. 90 *However terrible, their Lectures on Modern History*, 25, 60, 136, 193.

p. 90 *"produced no lasting"* "Sir Erskine," 71; see also 58; "Freedom in Christianity," 41; *Lectures on Modern History*, 25, 126, 143, 152, 161, 197–98. See Lazarski, *Power Tends to Corrupt*, 106–14.

p. 91 *The subsequent stages Lectures on Modern History*, 197; see also 25, 152.

p. 91 *"the era in which parties" Lectures on Modern History*, 198; see also 188–97, 200.

p. 92 *They appreciated the Lectures on Modern History*, 206; see also 106–8, 200; "Review of Thomas Arnold's *Manual of English Literature*," 145; "Review of Frederick Arnold's *Public Life of Lord Macaulay*," 153.

p. 92 *"Authority was limited and" Lectures on Modern History*, 221; "Sir Erskine," 72.

p. 93 *"liberty founded on" Lectures on the French Revolution*, 97; *Lectures on Modern History*, 221; "Sir Erskine," 81.

p. 93 *And it is mainly this Lectures on Modern History*, 208. Acton mentions on this occasion the speeches of Earl of Chatham (William Pitt the Elder, 1708–1778), Earl of Camden (Charles Pratt, 1714–1794), and Burke. See also "Review of Thomas Arnold's *Manual of English Literature*," 145; "Review of Frederick Arnold's *Public Life of Lord Macaulay*," 153–54; Lazarski, *Power Tends to Corrupt*, 115–23.

p. 93 *As for the Tories Lectures on Modern History*, 207.

p. 94 *In some of his letters* See p. 52 *He was, no doubt.*

p. 94 *Was this what prevented* See p. 55 *In England, the term.*

p. 95 *Fourth, colonial laws Lectures on Modern History*, 25, 191–93, 292; *Lectures on the French Revolution*, 21–22; "Colonies," 183–87; Lord Acton, "The

War in America," *Rambler*, n.s., 5 (September 1861), reprinted in *SWLA*, 1:288. See Lazarski, *Power Tends to Corrupt*, 126–30.

p. 95 *The Declaration of Independence* *Lectures on Modern History*, 287–93; *Lectures on the French Revolution*, 20–26; "Colonies," 187; "Freedom in Christianity," 49; Lord Acton to Lady Blennerhassett, April 22, 1887, and May 1887, *Correspondence*, 272–73 and 277–78; Lord Acton, "The American Commonwealth. By James Bryce," *English Historical Review* 4 (1889), reprinted in *SWLA*, 1:404. See Lazarski, *Power Tends to Corrupt*, 131–37.

p. 96 *The delegates did their* "Civil War in America," 268–72; "Political Causes," 219–23; *Lectures on the French Revolution*, 33–35; "The American Commonwealth. By James Bryce," 399–405.

p. 96 *Furthermore, the Bill* "Civil War in America," 263–67; "Political Causes," 223–31; *Lectures on the French Revolution*, 33–37; *Lectures on Modern History*, 295. See Lazarski, *Power Tends to Corrupt*, 138–42.

p. 97 *"I call their success unexampled"* "Civil War in America," 264. See *Lectures on Modern History*, 295; *Lectures on the French Revolution*, 37.

p. 97 *If America was for* "Freedom in Christianity," 43–44; "Nationality," 416–17; *Lectures on the French Revolution*, 160; Add. Mss. 4428, 43.

p. 98 *The Glorious Revolution* *Lectures on the French Revolution*, 1–33; "Expectation of the French Revolution," 38–52; "Sir Erskine," 73. See Lazarski, *Power Tends to Corrupt*, 177–83.

p. 99 *He also invited* *Lectures on the French Revolution*, 42–52; "Sir Erskine," 74.

p. 99 *As time went by* *Lectures on the French Revolution*, 57–80, 126–57, 174–90, 224–50.

p. 100 *In their place, it* *Lectures on the French Revolution*, 100–123, 164, 198–99. See Lazarski, *Power Tends to Corrupt*, 184–99.

p. 100 *"cleared away the history of France"* *Lectures on the French Revolution*, 198–99.

p. 100 *"The discussion of principles"* *Lectures on the French Revolution*, 200.

p. 100 *These drastic steps* *Lectures on the French Revolution*, 200–201, 205–6, 209, 213–14, 225–27, 231, 234–41. See Lazarski, *Power Tends to Corrupt*, 200–204.

p. 101 *It was these proconsuls* *Lectures on the French Revolution*, 226, 232, 234, 241–43, 250–53, 255–57, 260, 262–64, 268, 285, 287–88, 296–99, 324, 332. See Lazarski, *Power Tends to Corrupt*, 204–16; "Sir Erskine," 75.

p. 101 *The convention could* *Lectures on the French Revolution*, 226, 330–41.

p. 102 *The revolt of monarchists* *Lectures on the French Revolution*, 341–44. See Lazarski, *Power Tends to Corrupt*, 216–19.

p. 103 *The French Constitution* *Lectures on the French Revolution*, 100; 161, 258, 269–271; "Sir Erskine," 76; "Mr. Goldwin Smith's *Irish History*," 92–95; "Nationality," 410–11, 415, 418.

p. 103 *"The substance of the ideas"* "Nationality," 417.

p. 104 *"An absolute parliament"* "The Piedmontese Ultimatum to the Holy See," 463; "Cavour," 441. See p. 103 *The French Constitution Lectures on the French Revolution*; Lazarski, *Power Tends to Corrupt*, 199–200.

p. 105 *In other words, Italy* See "Sir Erskine," 76–79; "The Piedmontese Ultimatum to the Holy See," 462–64; "Nationality," 415, 424, 429; "Cavour," 441–43; "The Revolution in Italy," 496–98.

p. 105 *These hopes were* "Nationality," 417–20.

p. 105 *Consequently, nationalism* "Nationality," 420–23.

p. 106 *"The theory of nationality"* See p. 58 *"more absurd and more criminal."*

p. 107 *Once the test* "Political Causes," 229–33; "Civil War in America," 269.

p. 107 *This strengthened the* "Political Causes," 232–39.

p. 107 *George Washington* "Political Causes," 247; "Civil War in America," 278.

p. 107 *For him, this was* "Political Causes," 223–33; "Civil War in America," 274–76; "The War in America," 293.

p. 108 *According to Acton* See p. 49 *He felt slavery*. For Acton's view on slavery in general, see Lazarski, *Power Tends to Corrupt*, 161–65.

p. 108 *The victorious presidential* "Political Causes," 237, 256–57; "Civil War in America," 275–76.

p. 109 *"They would have"* "Civil War in America," 277–78.

p. 109 *He interpreted it* "The War in America," 289.

p. 109 *"The secession of the Southern"* "Political Causes" (1861), 261–62.

p. 110 *"The South applied the principle"* "Civil War in America," 278.

p. 110 *"it is too soon to"* "Civil War in America," 278–79.

p. 110 *"And yet, by the development" Lectures on Modern History*, 295.

4. Reception and Legacy

p. 115 *He was still Letters of Lord Acton to Mary*, ix, lxiii. See Reginald L. Poole, "John Emerich, Lord Acton," *English Historical Review* 17, no. 68 (October 1902): 692–93; Gooch, *History and Historians in the Nineteenth Century*, 365.

p. 116 *These were the Cambridge* Chronologically, the first was the collection of his letters to Mary Drew (*Letters of Lord Acton to Mary*), published in 1904 and republished in a fuller edition in 1913. Because of its irreverent content relating to the Catholic Church and the papacy, in 1906 Abbot Gasquet published Acton's letters to Richard Simpson and Thomas F. Wetherell purged of any such irreverent remarks (*Lord Acton and His Circle* [London: G. Allen]). Two of Acton's former pupils—John Neville Figgis and Reginald Vere Laurence—were the editors of the remaining books printed in this early period. These were *Lectures on Modern History* (1906), *Historical Essays and Studies* (London: Macmillan, 1907), *The History of Freedom, and Other Essays* (London: Macmillan, 1907), *Lectures on the French Revolution* (1910), and *Selections from the Correspondence of the First Lord Acton* (1917).

p. 116 *If his knowledge of* Bryce, *Studies in Contemporary Biography*, 386–88; *Letters of Lord Acton to Mary*, xv.

p. 116 *"no Englishman has ever"* Grant Duff, *Out of the Past*, 1:171. Himmelfarb quotes several accounts confirming Acton's extraordinary erudition, including that of Bishop Mandell Creighton, who referred to him as "the most learned Englishmen now alive" (*Lord Acton*, 190–91).

p. 117 *"passed no judgment" Letters of Lord Acton to Mary*, lxiii–lxiv; *Selections from the Correspondence*, ix.

p. 117 *Thus, the question was The History of Freedom*, xi, xviii, xxiv–xxv. See *Letters of Lord Acton to Mary*, ix–x, lxiv; Bryce, *Studies in Contemporary Biography*, 390; Fisher, *Studies in History and Politics*, 89–91.

p. 117 *As mentioned, Acton* Hill, *Lord Acton*, 276.

p. 117 *As a result, he* Crane Brinton, "Lord Acton's Philosophy of History," *Harvard Theological Review* 12, no. 1 (January 1919): 88–90; Oliver H. Richardson, "Lord Acton and His Obiter Dicta on History," *The Sewanee Review* 13, no. 2 (April 1905): 134.

p. 117 *"He had none of the"* Brinton, "Lord Acton's Philosophy of History," 85, 91; Richardson, "Lord Acton and His Obiter Dicta on History," 133; Fisher, *Studies in History and Politics*, 98.

p. 118 *For were this view* Fisher, *Studies in History and Politics*, 95–96.

p. 118 *As mentioned in chapter* Lord Acton, *Essays in the Liberal Interpretation of History*, ed. William H. McNeill (Chicago and London: University of Chicago Press, 1967), xviii; David Ogg, *Herbert Fisher, 1865–1940: A Short Biography* (London: Edward Arnold, 1947), 166.

p. 118 *Like Ranke, he* "Inaugural Lecture on the Study of History," 17–41, especially 18, 22. Lord Acton, "German Schools of History," *English Historical Review* 1 (1886), reprinted in *SWLA*, 2:325, 331–34; Richardson, "Lord Acton and His Obiter Dicta on History," 131–34. See Chadwick, *Acton and History*, 212–17, 228.

p. 119 *In other words, he* "Inaugural Lecture on the Study of History," 38, 40–41; "German Schools of History," 331–33; *Lectures on the French Revolution*, 92; see Richardson, "Lord Acton and His Obiter Dicta on History," 132–34.

p. 119 *Its position did certainly* C. T. McIntire, *Herbert Butterfield: Historian as Dissenter* (New Haven, CT: Yale University Press, 2004), 22; Chadwick, *Acton and History*, 228, 245. See William H. McNeill's introduction to Acton's *Essays in the Liberal Interpretation of History*, xviii.

p. 119 *"The weight of opinion is"* "Inaugural Lecture on the Study of History," 38.

p. 119 *By the late 1920s and* See G. R. Elton, "Herbert Butterfield and the Study of History," *The Historical Journal* 27, no. 3 (September 1984): 731–32.

p. 120 *On the one hand* Elton, "Herbert Butterfield," 732–34.

p. 120 *"in Lord Acton, the Whig"* Herbert Butterfield, *The Whig Interpretation of History* (London: G. Bell and Sons, 1931), especially 5, 11, 30, 71–74, 109–20.

p. 120 *The attack was clever* Acton was not a Whig historian; see Harold Acton, "Lord Acton," *Chicago Review* 15, no. 1 (Summer 1961): 32; McNeill's introduction to Acton's *Essays in the Liberal Interpretation of History*, xviii–xix; David Mathew, *Lord Acton and His Time* (Tuscaloosa, AL: University of Alabama Press, 1968), 24; Hill, *Lord Acton*, 105; McIntire, *Herbert Butterfield: Historian as Dissenter*, 60.

p. 121 *In turn, Acton's* See Elton, "Herbert Butterfield," 732. Elton, Butterfield's younger colleague at Cambridge, was even surprised that he bothered to attack the "false history" that was "already passing away when he started to uncover it" and that he made Acton so prominent in his book (pp. 731–32).

p. 121 *"Old-fashioned historian"* Butterfield, *Man on His Past*, 81.

p. 122 *"in a sense Acton was"* Gooch, *History and Historians in the Nineteenth Century*, 366; Chadwick, *Acton and History*, 228.

p. 123 *But he was also* Fisher, *Studies in History and Politics*, 86–111, especially 91, 94, 97–101.

p. 124 *In his famous book* Friedrich A. Hayek, *The Road to Serfdom*, 1st ed. 1944 (Chicago: University of Chicago Press, 1980), 13–14, 70, 144, 183.

p. 124 *Thus, describing Acton* Friedrich A. Hayek, *Studies in Philosophy, Politics and Economics* (London: Routledge & Kegan Paul, 1967), 135–47, especially 141, 143. Hayek linked Acton's political thought to that of Jakob Burkhardt (a German) and Tocqueville to make it more appealing to the Germans. See Friedrich A. Hayek, *The Constitution of Liberty* (Chicago: University of Chicago Press, 1978), 408–10.

p. 124 *"did not wholly escape"* Hayek, *Studies in Philosophy, Politics and Economics*, 93–95. See Gertrude Himmelfarb, "The American Revolution in the Political Theory of Lord Acton," *Journal of Modern History* (Chicago) 21, no. 4 (December 1949): 293.

p. 125 *"The core of this movement"* Hayek, *New Studies in Philosophy, Politics, Economics and the History of Ideas*, 118–20. See also Hayek, *Studies in Philosophy, Politics and Economics*, 160–63.

p. 125 *Hayek's view of liberalism* Hayek, *Studies in Philosophy, Politics and Economics*, 94, 160–77.

p. 126 *In view of Acton's contempt* Himmelfarb, "The American Revolution in the Political Theory of Lord Acton," 293–94. See also Altholz, *The Conscience of Lord Acton*, 3.

p. 126 *"a prophet of our time"* See Lord Acton to Mary Gladstone, June 3, 1881, in *Letters of Lord Acton to Mary*, 83; Himmelfarb, *Lord Acton*, vii, 3.

p. 127 *"a minor prophet of"* See Gertrude Himmelfarb, "Introduction," in *Essays on Freedom and Power*, 7; G. P. Gooch, *Under Six Reigns* (London: Longmans, Green, 1958), 48; G. P. Gooch, *Historical Surveys and Portraits* (New York: Barnes & Noble, 1966), 156; Schuettinger, *Lord Acton*, 3, 10; Josef L.

Altholz, Damian McElrath, and James C. Holland, "Introduction," in *Acton-Simpson Correspondence*, 1:ix; Hugh Trevor-Roper, "Introduction," in *Lectures on Modern History*, 14.

p. 127 *The unwritten history* Kochan, *Acton on History*, 31–33.

p. 127 *Both use Acton's* Hill, *Lord Acton*, x.

p. 128 *"Too liberal to submit"* Josef L. Altholz, *The Liberal Catholic Movement in England: The "Rambler" and Its Contributors, 1848–1864* (London: Burns & Oates, 1962), 244.

p. 128 *again, an unlikely perspective* Mathew, *Lord Acton and His Time*, 47, 139–49; David Mathew, *Acton: The Formative Years* (London: Eyre & Spottiswoode, 1946).

p. 129 *"by what they had published"* Chadwick stated it in his foreword to Hill, *Lord Acton*, xi.

p. 130 *"there has been"* Figgis and Laurence, "Introduction: Lord Acton as a Professor," x.

p. 130 *"if he aspires to be a judge"* Himmelfarb, *Lord Acton*, 199–200. She quotes these unfriendly reviews: *Spectator* 74 (1895): 807; *Saturday Review* 79 (1895): 922; and Henry C. Lea, "Ethical Values in History," in *Minor Historical Writing*, ed. A. C. Howland (Philadelphia, 1942), 60.

p. 131 *Hill judges it* Hill, *Lord Acton*, 381. "Review of Lea's *History of Inquisition*," *English Historical Review* 3 (1888): 773–788, reprinted in *SWLA*, 2:393–411.

p. 131 *"With greater moral courage"* Chadwick, *Acton and History*, 244.

p. 131 *There were also some* See Stephen J. Tonsor, "Lord Acton: Another Eminent Victorian" (a review of *Lord Acton* by Roland Hill), *Modern Age* 43, no. 3 (2001): 256; John Nurser, *The Reign of Conscience: Individual, Church, and State in Lord Acton's History of Liberty* (New York and London: Garland Publishing, 1987), 123; Christopher Clausen, "Lord Acton and the Lost Cause," *American Scholar* 69, no. 1 (Winter 2000): 50; Hill, *Lord Acton*, 180; Kochan, *Acton on History*, 88; E. D. Watt, "'Freedom' as an Incantation: The Example of Lord Acton," *Journal of Politics* 25, no. 3 (August 1963).

p. 132 *"honourable oblivion"* Elton, "Herbert Butterfield," 731. If Watt's and Elton's remarks on Acton border on derision, the short book by Hugh Tulloch (*Acton* [London: Weidenfeld & Nicolson, 1988]) is little more than a pamphlet whose evidence includes too many mistakes to be trusted.

p. 132 *Of these, two collections Briefwechsel*; *Acton-Simpson Correspondence*.

p. 132 *A few years later* Lord Acton, "Journal of Lord Acton: Rome, 1857," ed. Herbert Butterfield, *Cambridge Historical Journal* 8 (1946); *Lord Acton and the First Vatican Council: Journal*, ed. Edmund Campion (Sydney: Catholic Theological Faculty, 1975); *Acton in America: The American Journal of Sir John Acton, 1853* (1979).

p. 133 *Both "Lectures on Modern History"* Lord Acton, *Essays on Church and State*; *Lord Acton: The Decisive Decade, 1864–1874: Essays and Documents*, ed.

Damian McElrath (Louvain: Bibliothèque de l'Université & Publications Universitaires de Louvain, 1970); *Lectures on the French Revolution*, foreword by Stephen J. Tonsor (Indianapolis: Liberty Fund, 2000).

p. 133 *What is notable* "John Emerich Edward Dalberg, Lord Acton," OLL, https://oll.libertyfund.org/person/john-emerich-edward-dalberg-lord-acton.

p. 134 *"His message is one" SWLA*, 1:xviii.

p. 134 *"Perhaps after the horrors"* Hill, *Lord Acton*, 410.

Bibliography

Primary Sources

Unpublished

The Acton Papers, the Department of Manuscripts, Cambridge University Library (CUL). The CUL holds a full collection of Lord Acton's notes (Additional Manuscripts 4757–5021, 5381–5710). Some of it has been published in J. Rufus Fears, *Selected Writings of Lord Acton*, 3 vols. (Indianapolis: Liberty Classics, 1985–1988), 3:489–674 (referred to as *SWLA*), and George Watson, *Lord Acton's History of Liberty: A Study of His Library, with an Edited Text of His History of Liberty Notes* (Aldershot: Scolar Press, 1994), 56–107.

Published

Acton, John Emerich Edward Dalberg, Baron

Acton-Creighton Correspondence, April 5, 1887, Add. Mss. 6871. Reprinted in *SWLA*, 2:378–88.

Acton in America: The American Journal of Sir John Acton, 1853, see "Lord Acton's American Diaries."

Acton-Simpson Correspondence, see *The Correspondence of Lord Acton and Richard Simpson*.

Acton to Johann Joseph Ignaz von Döllinger, June 22, 1853, and September 6, 1853. In *Briefwechsel*, 1:27–29, 38.

Acton to Lady Blennerhassett, February 1879; April 22 and May 1887. In *Selections from the Correspondence of the First Lord Acton*, 54–56, 271–73.

Acton to Mary Gladstone, December 14, 1880; April 24 and June 3, 1881; February 20, 1882, and December 18, 1884. In *Letters of Lord Acton to Mary*, 31–38; 82–83; 97–98; 157–60.

"The American Commonwealth. By James Bryce." *English Historical Review* 4 (1889): 388–96. Reprinted in *SWLA*, 1:395–405.

"Cavour." *Rambler*, n.s., 5 (July 1861): 141–65. Reprinted in *SWLA*, 1:434–58.

"The Civil War in America: Its Place in History." *Bridgnorth Journal*, January 20, 1866. Reprinted in *SWLA*, 1:263–79.

"Colonies." *Rambler*, n.s., 6 (March 1863): 391–400. Reprinted in *SWLA*, 1:177–88.

"Conflicts with Rome." *Home and Foreign Review* 4 (April 1864): 667–96. Reprinted in *SWLA*, 3:234–59.

The Correspondence of Lord Acton and Richard Simpson. Edited by Josef L. Altholz, Damian McElrath, and James C. Holland. 3 vols. Cambridge: Cambridge University Press, 1971–1975.

"Döllinger on the Temporal Power." *Rambler*, n.s., 6 (November 1861): 1–62. Reprinted in *SWLA*, 3:67–127.

"Emancipation of the Serfs in Russia." *Rambler*, n.s., 3 (July 1860): 265–88. Reprinted in *SWLA*, 1:505–17.

Essays in the Liberal Interpretation of History. Edited by William H. McNeill. Chicago and London: University of Chicago Press, 1967.

Essays on Church and State. Edited by Douglas Woodruff. London: Hollis and Carter, 1952.

Essays on Freedom and Power. Edited by Gertrude Himmelfarb. 2nd ed. New York: Meridian Books, 1955.

"Expectation of the French Revolution." *Rambler*, n.s., 5 (July 1861): 190–213. Reprinted in *SWLA*, 2:38–62.

"German Schools of History." *English Historical Review* 1 (1886): 7–42. Reprinted in *SWLA*, 2:325–64.

"Hefele's Life of Ximenes." *Rambler*, n.s., 3 (July 1860): 158–70. Reprinted in *Essays on Church and State*, 386–87.

Historical Essays and Studies. Edited by John Neville Figgis and Reginald Vere Laurence. London: Macmillan, 1907.

The History of Freedom, and Other Essays. Edited by John Neville Figgis and Reginald Vere Laurence. London: Macmillan, 1907.

"The History of Freedom in Antiquity." An address delivered to the members of the Bridgnorth Institution at the Agricultural Hall, February 26, 1877. Reprinted in *SWLA*, 1:5–28.

"The History of Freedom in Christianity." An address delivered to the members of the Bridgnorth Institution at the Agricultural Hall, May 28, 1877. Reprinted in *SWLA*, 1:29–53.

"Inaugural Lecture on the Study of History." In *Lectures on Modern History*, 17–41.

"J. G. Phillimore's *History of England during the Reign of George III*." *Home and Foreign Review* 3, no. 6 (October 1863): 713. Reprinted in *Historical Essays and Studies*, 403–6.

"Journal of Lord Acton: Rome, 1857." Edited by Herbert Butterfield. *Cambridge Historical Journal* 8 (1946): 186–204.

Lectures on the French Revolution. Edited by Neville Figgis and Reginald Vere Laurence. London: Macmillan, 1910.

Lectures on Modern History. Edited by Hugh Trevor-Roper. 3rd ed. Cleveland and New York: Meridian Books, 1967.

Letters of Lord Acton to Mary, Daughter of the Right Hon. W. E. Gladstone. Edited by Herbert Paul. 2nd rev. ed. London: Macmillan, 1913.

Letters to the editor of *The Times*, November 8–December 9, 1874. Reprinted in *SWLA*, 3:363–84.

Lord Acton: The Decisive Decade, 1864–1874: Essays and Documents. Edited by Damian McElrath. Louvain: Bibliothèque de l'Université & Publications Universitaires de Louvain, 1970.

Lord Acton and His Circle. Edited by Abbot Gasquet. London: G. Allen, 1906.

Lord Acton and the First Vatican Council: Journal. Edited by Edmund Campion. Sydney: Catholic Theological Faculty, 1975.

"Lord Acton's American Diaries." First printed in *Fortnightly Review* 110 (November 1921): 727–42; 110 (December 1921): 917–34; and 111 (January 1922): 63–83. Reprinted as *Acton in America: The American Journal of Sir John Acton, 1853*. Edited by S. W. Jackman. Shepherdstown, WV: Patmos Press, 1979.

"Mr. Goldwin Smith's *Irish History*." *Rambler*, n.s., 6 (January 1862): 190–220. Reprinted in *SWLA*, 2:67–97.

"Nationality." *Home and Foreign Review* 1, no. 1 (July 1862): 1–25. Reprinted in *SWLA*, 1:409–33.

"Notes on the Present State of Austria." *Rambler*, n.s., 4 (January 1861): 193–205. Reprinted in *Essays on Church and State*, 339–45.

"The Piedmontese Ultimatum to the Holy See." *Rambler*, n.s., 6 (January 1862): 277–81. Reprinted in *SWLA*, 1:459–66.

"Political Causes of the American Revolution." *Rambler*, n.s., 5 (May 1861): 17–61. Reprinted in *SWLA*, 1:216–62.

"The Political System of the Popes." *Rambler*, n.s., 2 (January 1860): 154–65; 3 (May 1860): 27–38; and 4 (January 1861): 183–93. Reprinted in *Essays on Church and State*, 123–4.

"Political Thoughts on the Church." *Rambler*, n.s., 11 (January 1859): 30–49. Reprinted in *SWLA*, 3:17–36.

"The Protestant Theory of Persecution." *Rambler*, n.s., 6 (March 1862): 318–51. Reprinted in *SWLA*, 2:98–131.

"Reports on the Civil War in America." *Rambler* (January 1982): 280–92. Reprinted in *SWLA*, 1:280–360.

"Review of Frederick Arnold's *Public Life of Lord Macaulay*." *Home and Foreign Review* 2, no. 3 (January 1863): 257–60. Reprinted in *SWLA*, 1:151–55.

"Review of Hudson's *Second War of Independence in America.*" *Home and Foreign Review* 2 (April 1863): 656–58. Reprinted in *SWLA*, 1:368–71.
"Review of James Burton Robertson, *Lectures on Ancient and Modern History.*" *Rambler*, n.s., 2 (March 1860): 397. Reprinted in *SWLA*, 2:515–16.
"Review of Lea's *History of Inquisition.*" *English Historical Review* 3 (1888): 773–88. Reprinted in *SWLA*, 2:393–411.
"Review of Poirson's *Histoire du Règne de Henri IV.*" *Dublin Review* 44 (March 1858): 1–31. Reprinted in *SWLA*, 2:20.
"Review of Thomas Arnold's *Manual of English Literature.*" *Home and Foreign Review* 2, no. 3 (January 1863): 250–54. Reprinted in *SWLA*, 1:141–46.
"The Revolution in Italy." *Rambler*, n.s., 3 (July 1860): 273–81. Reprinted in *SWLA*, 1:491–501.
"The Roman Question." *Rambler*, n.s., 2 (January 1860): 136–54.
Selected Writings of Lord Acton. Edited by J. R. Fears. 3 vols. Indianapolis: Liberty Classics, 1985–1988.
Selections from the Correspondence of the First Lord Acton. Edited by John Neville Figgis and Reginald Vere Laurence. London: Longmans, Green, 1917.
"Sir Erskine May's *Democracy in Europe.*" *Quarterly Review* 145 (January 1878): 112–42. Reprinted in *SWLA*, 1:54–85.
"The States of the Church." *Rambler*, n.s., 2 (March 1860): 291–323. Reprinted in *Essays on Church and State*, 94–104.
SWLA, see *Selected Writings of Lord Acton*. "Venn's Life of St. Francis Xavier." *Home and Foreign Review* 2, no. 3 (January 1863): 172–89.
"The War in America." *Rambler*, n.s., 5 (September 1861): 424–32. Reprinted in *SWLA*, 1:286–99.

Other Authors

Briefwechsel, see Döllinger.
Döllinger, Johann Joseph Ignaz von. *Ignaz von Döllinger Briefwechsel, 1820–1890*. Edited by Victor Conzemius. 3 vols. Munich: Bayerischen Akademie der Wissenschaften, 1963–1981.

Secondary Sources

Acton, Harold. "Lord Acton." *Chicago Review* 15, no. 1 (Summer 1961): 31–44.
Altholz, Josef L. "The Conscience of Lord Acton." Houston: University of St. Thomas, 1970.
——. *The Liberal Catholic Movement in England: The "Rambler" and Its Contributors, 1848–1864*. London: Burns & Oates, 1962.
——. "Lord Acton and the Plan of the Cambridge Modern History." *Historical Journal* 39, no. 3 (September 1996): 723–36.

Altholz, Josef L., Damian McElrath, and James C. Holland, eds. *The Correspondence of Lord Acton and Richard Simpson*. 3 vols. Cambridge: Cambridge University Press, 1971–1975.

Bell, Duncan. "What Is Liberalism?" *Political Theory* 42, no. 6 (2014): 682–725.

Berlin, Isaiah. "The Birth of Greek Individualism." In *Liberty*, edited by Henry Hardy, 287–321. Oxford: Oxford University Press, 2005.

Brinton, Crane. "Lord Acton's Philosophy of History." *Harvard Theological Review* 12, no. 1 (January 1919): 84–112.

Bryce, James. *Studies in Contemporary Biography*. London and New York: Macmillan, 1903.

Butterfield, Herbert. *Man on His Past*. Cambridge: Cambridge University Press, 1979.

——. *The Whig Interpretation of History*. London: G. Bell and Sons, 1931.

Chadwick, Owen. *Acton and Gladstone*. London: Athlone Press, 1976.

——. *Acton and History*. Cambridge: Cambridge University Press, 2002.

Clark, G. N. "The Origin of the *Cambridge Modern History*." *Cambridge Historical Journal* 8 (1945): 57–64.

Clausen, Christopher. "Lord Acton and the Lost Cause." *American Scholar* 69, no. 1 (Winter 2000): 49–58.

Constant, Benjamin. *The Liberty of the Ancients Compared with That of Moderns* (1819). Accessed April 5, 2021. https://oll.libertyfund.org/title/constant-the-liberty-of-ancients-compared-with-that-of-moderns-1819.

Drew, Mary. *Acton, Gladstone and Others*. 2nd ed. Port Washington, NY: Kennikat Press, 1968.

Drozdowski, E., and H. Parker. "Lord Acton: A Prophet for This Generation?" *South Atlantic Quarterly* 3 (1953): 521–27.

Elton, G. R. "Herbert Butterfield and the Study of History." *Historical Journal* 27, no. 3 (September 1984): 729–43.

Figgis, John Neville, and Reginald Vere Laurence. "Introduction: Lord Acton as a Professor." In Acton, *Lectures on Modern History*. 1st ed., IX–XIX London: Macmillan, 1906.

Fisher, Herbert. *Studies in History and Politics*. Oxford: Clarendon Press, 1920.

Gladstone, William Ewart. *The Vatican Decrees in Their Bearing on Civil Allegiance: A Political Expostulation*. London: J. Murray, 1974.

Gooch, G. P. *Historical Surveys and Portraits*. New York: Barnes & Noble, 1966.

——. *History and Historian in the Nineteenth Century*. Boston: Beacon Press, 1959.

——. *Under Six Reigns*. London: Longmans, Green, 1958.

Grant Duff, Mountstuart E. *Out of the Past*. 2 vols. London: John Murray, 1903.

Hayek, Friedrich A. *The Constitution of Liberty*. Chicago: University of Chicago Press, 1978.

——. *New Studies in Philosophy, Politics, Economics and the History of Ideas*. London: Routledge & Kegan Paul, 1982.

——. *The Road to Serfdom*. Chicago: University of Chicago Press, 1980.
——. *Studies in Philosophy, Politics and Economics*. London: Routledge & Kegan Paul, 1967.
Hill, Roland. *Lord Acton*. New Haven, CT: Yale University Press, 2000.
Himmelfarb, Gertrude. "The American Revolution in the Political Theory of Lord Acton." *Journal of Modern History* (Chicago) 21, no. 4 (December 1949): 293–312.
——. *Lord Acton: A Study in Conscience and Politics*. Chicago: University of Chicago Press, 1962.
Howard, Thomas A. "A Question of Conscience: The Excommunication of Ignaz von Döllinger." *Commonweal*. September 29, 2014. https://www.commonwealmagazine.org/question-conscience.
Kochan, Lionel. *Acton on History*. London: Andre Deutsch, 1954.
Lally, F. E. *As Lord Acton Says*. Newport, RI: Remington Ward, 1942.
Lazarski, Christopher. "Lord Acton's 'Organic' Liberalism and His Best Practical Regime." *Catholic Social Science Review* 25 (2020): 101–19.
——. *Power Tends to Corrupt: Lord Acton's Study of Liberty*. DeKalb, IL: Northern Illinois University Press, 2012.
Lazarski, Krzysztof. "Liberty in Equality: Lord Acton's Teaching on Participatory Democracy." *Athenaeum* 63, no. 3 (2019): 7–21.
——. "Lord Acton a Polska" [Lord Acton and Poland]. *Myśl Ekonomiczna i polityczna* 52, no. 1 (2016): 251–88.
Lea, Henry C. "Ethical Values in History." In *Minor Historical Writing*, edited by A. C. Howland. Philadelphia, 1942.
Mathew, David. *Acton: The Formative Years*. London: Eyre & Spottiswoode, 1946.
——. *Lord Acton and His Time*. Tuscaloosa: University of Alabama Press, 1968.
McIntire, C. T. *Herbert Butterfield: Historian as Dissenter*. New Haven, CT: Yale University Press, 2004.
Nurser, John. *The Reign of Conscience: Individual, Church, and State in Lord Acton's History of Liberty*. New York and London: Garland Publishing, 1987.
Ogg, David. *Herbert Fisher, 1865–1940: A Short Biography*. London: Edward Arnold, 1947.
Pollock, John. "Lord Acton at Cambridge." *Independent Review* 2 (April 1904): 360–78.
Poole, Reginald L. "John Emerich, Lord Acton." *English Historical Review* 17, no. 68 (October 1902): 692–99.
Richardson, Oliver H. "Lord Acton and His Obiter Dicta on History." *The Sewanee Review*, 13, no. 2 (April 1905): 129–42.
Ruggiero, Guido de. *The History of European Liberalism*. Translated by R. G. Collingwood. London: Oxford University Press, 1927.

Sabine, George H. *A History of Political Theory*. 4th ed. Hinsdale, IL: Dryden Press, 1973.

Schuettinger, Robert L. *Lord Acton: Historian of Liberty*. LaSalle, IL: Open Court, 1976.

Tocqueville, Alexis de. *Democracy in America*. Translated and edited by Harvey C. Mansfield and Delba Winthrop. Chicago: University of Chicago Press, 2000.

Tonsor, Stephen, J. "Lord Acton: Another Eminent Victorian." *Modern Age* 43, no. 3 (2001): 253–57.

Tulloch, Hugh. *Acton*. London: Weidenfeld & Nicolson, 1988.

"Vatican Council: The Question of Papal Infallibility." In *New Advent: Catholic Encyclopedia*. Accessed August 5, 2019. http://www.newadvent.org/cathen/15303a.htm.

Vögelin, Eric. "Liberalism and Its History." *Review of Politics* 36, no. 4 (October 1974): 506–7.

Watson, George. *Lord Acton's History of Liberty: A Study of His Library, with an Edited Text of His History of Liberty Notes*. Aldershot: Scolar Press, 1994.

Watt, E. D. "'Freedom' as an Incantation: The Example of Lord Acton." *Journal of Politics* 25, no. 3 (August 1963): 461–71.

Index

absolutism, 5, 88–89; French, 97–99, 103, 111; resistance to, 89–94, 111; state, 66, 134
Acton, Baron John Emerich Edward Dalberg: in America, 16; and the Catholic Church, 2, 9–14, 17–18, 21–30, 86, 118, 131; and Christianity, 21, 23, 77; as an editor and writer, 8, 17, 24–29, 126–127; early years of, 13, 15; foreign trips of, 15–17; and the history of liberty, 3, 7–10, 30–31, 37, 70, 112–113, 117; as landowner, 19; libraries of, 14, 30, 33, 120, 129; as the lord-in-waiting, 33; and moral judgment, 31–32, 118–119; in Munich, 13–15, 31; negative evaluation of, 115, 117, 119–123, 127, 130–132, 157n132; on papacy, 15, 24–25, 29, 118, 128; as a prophet, 2, 4, 66, 126–127, 129, 133, 141–142; in the Parliament, 17–19; positive evaluation of, 1–2, 116–119, 122–130, 133–134; and passion for books, 14, 19, 33, 115, 135; and putting off his writing, 30–33, 119, 122; as Regius Professor, 33–36; stern morality of, 31, 117, 119–121, 131; as a Whig historian, 120–125; and wife and children, 13, 19–20
Aldenham, 12, 14, 15, 19, 32
Alexander II, Tsar of Russia, 17
America: colonies in, 41–42, 48, 93–95, 98; democracy in, 5, 8, 48–50, 58–59, 96–97, 106, 109–110; federalism in, 42, 48–49, 96–97, 107–108, 110, 122; liberalism in, 6, 49–50, 56, 95; revolution in, 8, 42, 48, 94–95, 98, 102, 110, 137; slavery in, 42, 49, 58, 97, 107, 108. *See also* liberty: American vs. English notion of
Anabaptists, 90
ancien regime, 21, 46, 54, 98, 101, 102. *See also* absolutism
Anglicans, 22, 89, 91
Aquinas, St. Thomas, 84
Arco-Valley, Countess Marie von, 13, 19
Arco-Valley, Count Maximilian von, 13
Arianism, 81
aristocracy (nobility), 12–13, 48, 60, 83, 92, 98, 110. *See also* Whigs
Aristotle, 7, 74, 141
Armenians, 90
Augsburg, 26
Austria, 100, 123
Austro-Hungary, 27

Bentham, Jeremy, 53
Berlin, Isaiah, 123

best practical regime, 16, 59, 64, 68, 71, 106, 140
Bill of Rights, 47–48, 96
Bulgaria, 78
Burke, Edmund, 14, 93, 126, 131
Byzantium (Eastern Roman Empire), 77, 78, 82–84, 88. *See also* government: Byzantine (Muscovite)

Calhoun, John C., 61, 149n56
Calvinists, 89, 90. *See also* Puritans
Cambridge University, 7, 8, 12, 32–36
Carlow, 17, 18
Catholic Church: corruption in, 29, 77, 86, 88, 135–136; in England, 17–18, 22, 25, 27–28, 91; and liberalism, 21–27, 29–30, 90, 113, 127–128; and liberty, 43, 56, 87–90, 118, 131, 135, 139, 147n43–44; and persecution, 24, 72, 89, 90
Catholic periodicals, 8, 24–25, 27, 126
Charlemagne, Emperor of the Romans, 79, 82
Charles I, King of England, 92–93
Charles II, King of England, 92
Chronicle, 24–25
Church Council: First Vatican, 24–25, 27, 29–30, 132; of Nicaea, 81
citizens (citizenry), 27, 62, 71, 95, 110, 125; in antiquity, 72–76; and feudalism, 80; and liberty, 1, 3, 14, 42–45, 63, 67–67, 137–140; passive, 6, 54–55, 139
civic liberty: in America, 6, 16, 42, 47–48, 50, 95, 97, 106–107, 108; communal dimension of, 42, 63, 71, 113, 138–139; early modern, 6, 89; medieval, 6, 98, 113; roots of, 71, 73–75; threats to, 55–56, 64, 66, 136
civil liberty, 4, 43, 48, 93, 110
civil rights, 6, 42, 47–48, 53, 63–64, 96, 139
Civil War, American, 49, 106, 108–110, 126, 131–132
colonies. *See* America: colonies in
communism, 66, 126, 133–134, 141
Concordat of Worms, 83
Congress of Vienna, 21, 57, 105
conscience, 9, 43, 86, 87; freedom of, 43, 76, 147n44; and liberty, 14, 32, 43–45, 66, 138
Constantinople, 77, 114
constitution, 6, 39, 49, 101, 107–108, 120; of 1791, 54, 99, 101–104; Jacobin, 101. *See also* US Constitution
constitutionalism, 59, 93
constitutional law, 41, 53, 59
contractarian theory, 53, 98, 114
Counter-Reformation, 85, 88
cuius regio eius religio, 88

Dalberg, Duke Emmerich Joseph, 12
Dalberg, Marie Luisa, 13
Dalberg-Acton, Richard Ferdinand, 12
Danton, Georges, 101
Declaration of Independence, 95
Declaration of the Rights of Man and Citizens, 100, 147n41
democracy: in Athens, 59–60, 73–74; balanced (limited), 3, 48, 59, 68, 73–74, 96, 97, 129, 134, 140; as the best regime, 6, 68, 140; liberal, 11, 67, 134, 137; and liberty, 5–6, 8, 58–60, 62, 68; and national tradition, 60, 68, 69; and power, 3, 5, 60, 69, 75, 106, 141, 142; unlimited (absolute, pure), 9, 58–59, 64–69, 73–74, 103, 109–110, 117, 122–123, 141; vices of, 4–5, 59–62, 65–66, 68–69, 74, 114, 140–142; as the worst regime, 6, 65–66, 122, 134, 140–141. *See also* America: democracy in
Descartes, René, 124
despotism, 7, 75; democratic, 60, 101, 123, 142; Roman, 112; state, 9, 77, 84, 88, 111–112, 114. *See also* soft despotism
divine law. *See* natural law

divine right, 84, 93, 148n45
Döllinger, Ignaz von, 13–16, 19, 21, 23, 26, 29–30, 132

Elizabeth I, Queen of England, 28
England, 12, 16, 33–36, 50–51, 88, 115–118, 12–121, 124; boarding school in, 13; Catholic Church in, 18, 21–22, 25, 28, 118, 127; constitutionalism in, 47, 49, 59, 84, 93, 120; mature liberty in, 58, 93; religious and political conflicts in, 89–93, 95, 118; tradition of, 22, 46, 80, 109; Whiggism in, 48, 55, 93, 117, 125. *See also* liberty: American vs. English notion of; liberalism: English
Enlightenment, 21, 125
equality, 6, 9, 47–50, 53, 59, 93, 97, 103, 114; abstract, 2, 49, 64, 66; and democracy, 65, 122, 123; and inequality, 21, 47, 59, 93, 96, 109, 111–113, 139; legal, 28, 59, 64, 68, 100, 123; and nationalism, 105; and revolution, 102
Estates-General, 98–99
Europe, 15, 31, 33, 49, 54, 103–105, 109, 133; continental, 6, 106, 114, 123, 136; early modern, 88–89; east-central, 129; governments in, 21, 27; medieval, 82–84; nineteenth-century, 64; twentieth-century, 65

federalism, 62. *See also* America: federalism in
feudalism, 5, 7880, 82–83
Feuillants, 100
France, 27, 55, 57, 64, 66, 90, 97, 101–102, 104–105, 113; Estates-General in, 84; liberal Catholics in, 26; National Assembly in, 99, 100
French constitution of 1791. *See* constitution
French Revolution, 21, 85, 91, 103, 109, 111; crimes of, 8, 101–102; impact of, 54, 64, 102, 104, 114, 123, 125, 136–137; and nationalism, 57, 81, 105

general will, 134
Germanic tribes (Teutons), 78–79, 82; conversion to Christianity of, 81
Germany, 26, 57, 84, 105, 123, 124
Girondins, 100, 101
Gladstone, William E., 18, 19, 27, 28
Glorious Revolution, 46, 47, 91, 92, 93, 98, 113, 137
government: ancient, 73–76; armed resistance to, 83, 90, 92–93; Byzantine (Muscovite), 77, 82, 84, 88; central (national), 3, 39, 42, 48–49, 54–56, 97–98, 103, 106–108, 114, 139; constitutional, 21, 93, 96; local, 42, 48, 68, 96, 112; fragmentation of, 78–79, 81–82, 112; intelligent (efficient), 7–9, 74, 74, 88–89; limited, 41–47, 56, 60–62, 67, 83, 94, 96–97, 102, 104; representative, 47, 66–68, 84, 123, 140; unlimited (absolute), 5–6, 9, 23, 39, 54–66, 100, 103–110, 141. *See also* state
Great Britain. *See* England
Greece, ancient, 72–75, 88
Greeks, 73, 74, 76, 140

Habeas Corpus Act, 84
Harvard University, 16
Hayek, Friedrich von, 55, 123, 125
Hebrew. *See* Israel; liberty: Hebrew notion of
Hegel, Georg Wilhelm Friedrich, 124
Herrnsheim, 12, 15, 33
higher law (divine, natural), 52, 59, 67, 72, 74–75, 95, 111, 113, 139; as the highest principle, 6, 32, 40–41, 137; and liberty, 9, 39–41, 44–45; as natural law, 6, 41, 46, 52, 71, 93, 95, 138; secularization of, 41
Hitler, Adolf, 124
Hobbes, Thomas, 51, 53, 65, 92
Holy Roman Empire, 82
Home and Foreign Review, 18, 24
Huguenots, 28, 90, 113

inalienable rights, 53, 71, 98, 100, 110
individual rights, 3, 43–45, 53, 63, 67–68, 74, 105–106, 123, 138. *See also* rights of man
intermediary institutions, 42, 54, 55, 59, 63, 65, 67, 103, 141
investiture of the clergy, 82, 83
Ireland, 17, 18
Israel, ancient, 39–40, 46, 71–72, 76, 77, 90, 113. *See also* liberty: Hebrew notion of
Italy, 19, 22, 57, 64, 82, 84, 104, 105

Jacobins, 100–101
James II, King of England, 92
Jefferson, Thomas, 106–107
Jews. *See* Israel, ancient
Johnson, Andrew, 110
Judaism, 76

laissez-faire, 50, 51, 68
Lee, General Robert E, 110
Legislative Assembly, 100
Levenson-Gower, George, Second Earl Granville, 15–17
liberalism: constructivist (continental, doctrinaire), 3, 38–42, 50–57, 62–67, 86, 100, 103–106, 112–114, 117, 124–126, 137–138, 140–141; English, 22, 47, 48, 49, 52, 91–94, 124, 125; evolutionary (organic, Anglo-American), 6, 48–52, 56–59, 62, 67–68, 71, 94–97, 106–109, 113, 123–127, 137–138; and liberty, 1, 3, 6, 11, 38, 45, 52, 55, 110–111; and national liberty, 59, 63, 68, 105–106; and national tradition, 3, 48, 49–50, 52, 54, 68, 72, 113; and popular sovereignty, 5, 49, 113, 139; and property, 50–51; religious roots of, 77, 84, 89–91, 112–113, 136, 139. *See also* Acton: and the Catholic Church; civic liberty; civil liberty
liberty: American vs. English notion of, 47–48, 59, 93, 113; definition of, 37–45, 117, 138; and equality, 2, 6, 9, 53, 65, 96, 102–105, 114, 122; Hebrew notion of, 39–40, 71, 111, 139; as the highest political end, 6, 38–39, 43–46, 52, 55, 62, 67–68, 137; invisible hand of, 67; “mature,” 46–49, 52, 58, 66–67, 74, 93–96, 111–113, 137–139; and national tradition, 40, 41, 44, 46–47, 67, 72, 111; and religion, 41, 71, 77, 84, 88, 90–91, 134, 135. *See also* Catholic Church: and liberty; civic liberty; civil liberty; self-government
Locke, John, 53, 84, 90, 93
Lombards, 81
Louis XVI, 98
Luther, Martin, 88

Macaulay, Thomas Babington, 14, 93
Machiavelli, Niccolò, 9, 74, 85, 87, 88, 117
Magna Carta, 46
Manning, Archbishop Henry E., 22, 29
Marsilius of Padua, 84, 87
Marx, Karl, 124
Middle Ages. *See* feudalism; government: fragmentation of
Mill, John Stuart, 43, 53, 61
Milton, John, 90, 93
monarchy, 40, 60–61, 71–74, 80, 90, 92, 100–101, 113; constitutional monarchy, 99; unlimited (absolute), 64, 71, 85, 88–89, 93, 99, 103, 111, 114
Montesquieu, Charles-Louis de, 84, 124
morality, 18, 43, 44, 45, 67; in evaluating history, 31–32, 34, 44, 70, 87, 117–121, 124, 126–127, 130–131; and evil, 4–5, 24, 28, 86, 133; in politics, 53, 63–68, 71, 87–89, 117, 122, 133–134, 138–140; and religion, 27, 28, 32, 44, 86; Victorian, 20
moral law. *See* higher law
Munich, 12, 13, 14, 15, 21, 31

Napoleon I, 12, 57, 102, 105, 111
nation: based on rights, 57, 96; redefinition of, 136; as a spiritual community, 63

National Assembly, 99–100, 102, 103
National Convention, 101–102
nationalism, 56–58, 105–106, 126; birth of, 5, 57, 105; and the French Revolution, 57, 105; and liberalism, 5, 22, 105; and liberty, 39, 57–58; and minorities, 56–58, 63; and multinational state, 56–57, 63, 68, 80; as "national liberty," 56, 63, 140; as "national unity," 57–58, 105
national rights, 56–57, 105
National Socialism, 66
national tradition. *See* democracy: and national tradition; liberalism: and national tradition; liberty: and national tradition
natural law. *See* higher law
natural rights theory. *See* contractarian theory
Netherlands, 90
Newman, Cardinal John Henry, 22
New York, 16
North British Review, 24, 25, 27

Octavian Augustus, 75
oligarchy, 72, 75, 114
Oscott, 13
Ottoman Empire, 57
Oxford Movement, 21, 22, 24, 25

papacy, 21–24, 27–28, 81–83, 86–88, 118, 136, 154n116
papal infallibility, 26–28, 127
Papal States, 15, 22
Paris, 101
Parliament, 22, 47, 54, 62, 64, 84, 92–95, 104
Peloponnesian War, 59
Pericles, 59
Persian Empire, 73, 81
philosophes, 21, 53, 98, 125
Pitt (the Elder), William, Earl of Chatham, 152n93
Pius V, Pope St., 28
Pius IX, Pope, 21, 25, 27, 128
Plato, 8, 74
polis, 72–75, 113
Polybius, 75
Popper, Karl, 123
Pratt, Charles, Earl of Camden, 152n93
Presbyterians, 90–91
Protestantism. *See* Reformation
Protestant sects, 72, 86, 89–91, 95, 113
Providence, 44–45, 113
provincial rights, 54, 80, 102–103, 112
Puritans, 90–91, 94

Quakers, 90–91, 94

Rambler, 8, 18, 24–25, 27
Ranke, Leopold von, 118
Reformation, 22, 24, 90–91, 94, 103, 117; and liberty, 87–88, 118, 136
religion: autonomy of, 9, 76; dissenting to, 76, 89, 113; hostility to, 12, 54, 61, 136; and morality, 18, 28, 87; state, 62, 76, 82, 88; wars of, 85, 88, 90, 91, 111, 112, 136. *See also* liberty: and religion
Renaissance, 23, 35, 55, 85–86, 116
rights of Englishman, 48, 91, 93, 95
rights of man, 43, 53, 57–58, 71, 91–93, 95, 100, 136. *See also* individual rights
rights of minorities, 56, 59, 59, 63, 96
rights of the community, 3, 42, 63, 65, 138
Robespierre, Maximilien, 101
Roman Empire, 64, 76, 77, 79, 81, 117; fall of, 77, 81, 111–112
Roman Republic, 48, 75, 113
Rome, 15, 22, 26–28, 31, 132; ancient, 75–77, 97, 113, 140; aristocracy in, 83; law, 77–78; people of, 75
Roundheads, 93
Rousseau, Jean-Jacques, 90, 124
Russia (Muscovy), 17, 46, 57, 66, 77, 84, 123

Saint Petersburg, 17
Scientific Revolution, 85, 86

Selden, John, 93
self-government, 9, 14, 41–48, 66–68, 74, 82, 88, 95, 110–112, 139–140
separation of church and the state. *See* state: and the church
September Massacres, 101
Seven Years' War, 95
slavery, 75, 84, 85, 86, 97, 107, 108; and higher law, 41. *See also* America: slavery in
social engineering, 2, 3, 39, 55, 67, 138
socialism, 10, 50, 51, 58, 106, 131
society of estates, 21, 54, 78–79, 81, 88–89, 97–99, 103
Socinians, 90
Socrates, 76
soft despotism, 66, 68, 141
Solon, 72, 78
Somers, Baron John, 93
sovereignty: as democratic tyranny, 49, 54, 59–60, 73, 93, 136; and nationalism, 105–106; of the people, 6, 42, 47, 59–60, 71, 81, 88–90, 113, 136, 139–140; state, 42, 104, 107
Spain, 54, 57
Spring of Nations, 21, 105
state: ancient, 76–78, 140; and the church, 5, 9, 23, 76–77, 81–85, 87–91, 113, 135–136; and democracy, 62–69, 140, 141; and federalism, 48, 49, 96–97; medieval, 78–81; modern, 3, 48, 60, 65–68, 85–94, 97–110, 133, 140; multinational, 56–57; and nationalism, 57–58, 105–106; omnipotence of, 54–55; rights, 48–49, 96–97, 107, 110; and society, 42, 62–65
state of nature, 71; and abolishing the past, 54–55; as product of abstraction, 52–54, 114; scientific claims for, 53
St. Bartholomew's Day, 28, 90

taxes: in America, 16, 95, 107, 108; in France, 98; in the Middle Ages, 80, 81, 83, 84
Tegernsee, 13, 36
Thermidorian reaction, 101
Third Estate, 99
Tocqueville, Alexis, 3, 8, 54, 56, 61, 66, 68, 98, 123–124; as Acton's mentor, 14, 108
Tories (Tory), 18, 91, 93, 94, 125
totalitarianism. *See* democracy: as the worst regime
tyranny. *See* democracy: unlimited

US Constitution, 6, 48, 96–97, 107–108, 110, 122, 147n41
utilitarianism, 53, 63, 71, 141; as the greatest happiness for the greatest number, 53, 63

Vatican Council. *See* Church Council
Victoria, Queen, 12, 16, 17, 19, 33
voting rights, 6, 47, 50, 58–59, 93, 104, 139

Washington, George, 107
Whigs (Whiggism), 14–15, 17, 22, 48, 52, 55, 84, 91–94, 113, 117
William, Prince of Orange (William III, King of England), 92
Wiseman, Cardinal Nicholas, 18, 22, 24, 25
Worms, 12, 83